The Colosseum Critical Introduction
to David Mason

COLOSSEUM BOOKS

James Matthew Wilson, series editor

The Colosseum Critical Introduction

—————————————— to ——————————————

David Mason

Gregory Dowling

FRANCISCAN UNIVERSITY PRESS

Franciscan University Press
1235 University Boulevard
Steubenville, OH 43952
740-283-3771

Distributed by:
The Catholic University of America Press
c/o HFS
P.O. Box 50370
Baltimore, MD 21211
800-537-5487

Library of Congress Cataloging-in-Publication Data
Names: Dowling, Gregory, author.
Title: The Colosseum critical introduction to
David Mason / Gregory Dowling.
Other titles: Introduction to David Mason
Description: Steubenville, OH : Franciscan University
Press, [2022] |
Series: Colosseum books | Includes bibliographical
references.
Identifiers: LCCN 2022029429 |
ISBN 9781736656150 (paperback)
Subjects: LCSH: Mason, David, 1954—
Criticism and interpretation. |
LCGFT: Literary criticism.
Classification: LCC PS3563.A7879 Z66 2022 |
DDC 811/.54—dc23/eng/20220914
LC record available at https://lccn.loc.gov/2022029429

Cover Design by Kachergis Book Design
Cover Image: © akg-images/jh-Lightbox_Ltd./
John Hios
Printed in the United States of America.

Contents

Author's Note
vii

CHAPTER 1
Introduction
1

CHAPTER 2
Biography
20

CHAPTER 3
Buried Houses
26

CHAPTER 4
The Country I Remember
47

CHAPTER 5
Arrivals
68

CHAPTER 6
Ludlow
101

CHAPTER 7
Sea Salt
125

CHAPTER 8
Davey McGravy
156

CHAPTER 9
Words for Music
164

CHAPTER 10
The Sound
171

CHAPTER 11
Interview
196

Bibliography
217

Author's Note

This is a revised and extended version of the short book published by Story Line Press in 2013. It contains new chapters on David Mason's books published since then (in particular, his recent collections *Sea Salt* and *The Sound*) and examines the development of his career in new areas, above all in children's verse and opera libretti. The biographical chapter takes into consideration his career over the past nine years, focusing on the major change in his life: his marriage to the Australian poet Cally Conan-Davies and his subsequent move to Tasmania. The interview at the end of the book continues the conversation begun in 2013.

The Colosseum Critical Introduction to David Mason

CHAPTER 1

Introduction

In his first book of poems, *The Buried Houses*, David Mason dedicates a memorial poem to the writer and traveler Bruce Chatwin, declaring how he "envied [him] the life of worn-out-boots, / the way [he] exercised ideas by walking." The envy finds open expression at the end of the poem in the form of a wishful infinitive:

> To get out of a car, thank the driver
> and sling the moment's household on your back,
> looking ahead at open roads and fields
> no crows darken ... (14)

Interestingly, these lines are echoed in Mason's autobiographical work, *News from the Village*, when he recalls his own youthful travels in Europe:

A few months later I got out of a stranger's car somewhere in the Scottish border country, thanked the driver for the ride, slung my household on my back and started walking: it was a long walk: much of the time from January to July 1975 I was on the road, with brief residencies in London and Paris and Spain. A self-styled down-and-outer, nearly always alone, never letting friendships get below the surface, I loved the exhilaration of an empty road stretching ahead of me. (149)

The merest glance at the contents pages of his various volumes reveals how important travel has always been for Mason. *Arrivals*, for example, contains poems set in Greece, India, Ireland, New Zealand, and Scotland, in addition to the western and eastern states of America. Some of the poems in his books are clearly autobiographical, reporting his own travels for the purposes of study, pleasure, curiosity, or work; others feature a range of restless characters, whether the hucksters of "The Next Place," the exiled "Old Brit" stranded in Greece, the forlorn tour guide Mrs. Finn of "The Nightingales of Andritsena," sleepless Edward Lear in San Remo, or Maggie Gresham, who had wandering "in [her] blood." The main character in his verse novel *Ludlow* is in Colorado more or less by chance and dreams of his homeland, Crete.

The image of the "household on my back" is intriguing and helps to remind us that the theme of travel in his works is balanced by an equal emphasis on that of home. A simple glance at the titles of his poems is revelatory in this sense: "The Buried Houses," "All Houses Are Haunted," "Old House," "Three Characters from a Lost Home," "In the Borrowed House," "The Lost House," and "Home Care." In his poems, people seem to be perpetually on the move, while remembering or yearning for a lost childhood

home. In an early poem, he recalls playing on the beach under the distracted eye of an adult, his parents having "gone
where parents go," and he recounts how he "crawled inside
a rack of driftwood, / pretending it was home" ("In the
Islands," *The Buried Houses*). The image of a home of driftwood is a telling one. In his autobiographical writings and
interviews, Mason has acknowledged the traumatic effect
of his family's breakup when he was 12 and of his mother's
subsequent alcoholism, which led to his "fleeing domes-
ticity, traveling restlessly" (*Connotation Press* interview).
In *News from the Village*, he says in an offhand parenthesis,
"In high school I considered Eugene O'Neill's *Long Day's
Journey into Night*, with its drug-addicts and late-night so-
liloquies, to be my family's story, my fate" (147).

Andrew Frisardi, in the best essay yet written on Mason's poetry, declares that "since his earliest collection, *The
Buried Houses* (1991), David Mason has been making poetry out of his family roots." Frisardi points to the numerous different ways in which this theme informs his poetry,
from poems about his close family circle to ones about
distant ancestors. The personal ones are dotted throughout his books, reflecting on the various events that have affected the family, from his parents' separation and divorce
in 1968–69 to his brother's death in a climbing accident
at the age of 28, when the poet himself was 24, and later
poems reflecting on the problems of his parents' old age,
particularly his father's Alzheimer disease.

While acknowledging that his own early rootlessness

was caused by that of his parents, Mason has also declared that the chaos of his family perhaps pushed him in the opposite direction, in search of "tradition and stability in the world" (*News from the Village*, 22). It also drove him in search of deeper family roots, exploring both sides of his family background. In an essay in *The Poetry of Life*, he tells of his "genealogical obsessions," recounting the story of a family reunion in Colorado, during which he procured as many family documents as he could. Colorado for many years provided a more or less fixed point in his restless peregrinations around the world. Although he was born and grew up in Washington State, his childhood was punctuated by frequent visits to Colorado, where numerous relatives on his father's side lived. Mason subsequently studied for his first degree at Colorado College, and in 1998, twenty years after taking that degree, he took up a teaching position there, a position he held until his retirement in 2020. The city of Trinidad, where his grandfather and uncles lived, has proved of especial importance, returning in poems and essays and especially in his verse novel, *Ludlow*. A key poem in this sense is the one devoted to the river that flows through the town, which also provides the title, "El Rio de las Animas Perdidas en Purgatorio," ending with the wry lines, "My people's time beside the Purgatoire / was brief—far briefer than our scattering" (*The Country I Remember*, 59).

Mason has made it his business to bring together the scattered elements of his family history, and to do this, he

has relied most crucially on oral accounts. In an interview with David Rothman in *Able Muse*, Mason declared that he "grew up with wonderful storytellers," and that is partly why "other peoples' lives and histories have obsessed" him. His narrative poems frequently have their roots in his family history, and Mason has always been happy to talk about these personal connections. In the afterword to *Ludlow*, he declares, "The voices of my grandfather Abraham and his four sons still sound in my head. They are the most powerful influences on my writing life—as powerful as any book" (225).

Such influences are not exclusively western; Mason has always made much of the Scottish side of his heritage as well. It was no accident that his European travels began in Scotland. In a prose "Interlude" toward the end of *Ludlow*, he recounts how his grandfather, Abraham Mason, joined a Scots-Canadian regiment in the First World War and got himself wounded at Amiens. Mason "visited the regimental headquarters at Fort George near Inverness, and the kind old man who kept the records found his name in their big books and photocopied the pages" for him (199). In *Ludlow*, he beautifully evokes the nostalgia of the Scottish miner Too Tall Macintosh, who regrets that he and his wife "never made it back to Ayrshire, / never again declared a day was soft, / a Sunday not for laboring" (126).

In such nostalgic evocations, Masons also drew upon his second wife's Scottish connections, in particular memories of his father-in-law, John Lennox. This impressive figure lived half his life in the United States, but "whenever he used the word 'home' he meant Scotland, particularly Ayrshire" (*Connotation Press* interview). John Lennox was also cherished for his great oral gifts, in particular his stock of memorized dialect poetry: "He had border ballads, children's rhymes, English classics like Gray's 'Elegy'—the stuff they made him get at school, though he had quit school at a young age and gone to work in the steel mill. More than anything else, he had Burns" (*Connotation Press* interview).

Such feats of memory are a reproach to what Mason has referred to, in an essay on poetry of the American West, "the amnesia of the dominant culture" (*Two Minds*, 39). It is impossible to exaggerate how important the theme of memory is in Mason's poetry. Frisardi points to the trauma of the loss of his brother as a fundamental reason for Mason's treasuring "the phantasmagoric quality of memory that preserves the dead and the fleeting." One does not have to look far to see just how personal a theme this is for Mason; it also helps to explain the deeply felt anguish in his poems on his father's Alzheimer disease. As the quotation from Mason's essay on poetry of the West suggests, however, there is also a broader and more public dimension to his insistence on the theme of memory. It is as if Mason sees American culture itself as suffering from a kind of collective Alzheimer disease; poetry offers one form of counter-treatment.

In his prose memoir, *News from the Village*, Mason

presents the reader with the story of his growing awareness of the crucial importance of a sense of history. Although the subtitle of the book, *Aegean Friends*, suggests that it is primarily an account of people encountered in his various visits to Greece, it is perhaps more importantly a moving tale of personal growth. At the start of the book, Mason and his first wife, Jonna, are known to the neighbors in the Greek village where they are staying as *ta paidia*, "the children." Midway through the book comes the realization that "it was high time we grew up" (125). This process of maturation is to a large extent political: "I had walked through that village for more than a year, blissfully unaware who was a Fascist, who a Communist, a Royalist, a Socialist, a New Democrat. I had lived as if politics did not matter, which is the height of childishness" (126). There is the clear suggestion that such naivety is peculiarly American: "Once at the evening meal we were watching news of a minor incident on one of the islets off Turkey, and partly testing my Greek on a political subject, I ventured the very American opinion that the past was past and the two countries had better start anew and learn to live together" (177).

Although Mason does declare that "America's willingness to forget the past has sometimes been a blessing" (240), the primary movement in his memoir is toward an awareness that this kind of historical amnesia can be catastrophically perilous: "every now and then we learn of people who hate us enough to kill us. We can't remember why this is so, and we have to learn all over again about the world beyond the oceans" (240). This helps to explain what one might call the public dimension of his poetry. Memory is important not just in personal or family matters, but also in the broader fields of politics and history. In his interview with David Rothman, he states, "I never set out to be a poet of history, but it seems to have happened, at least in my narrative and dramatic efforts" (*Able Muse*, 138). He points to the influence of Anthony Hecht and Seamus Heaney, "both poets with an acute sense of history and therefore a gravity and purpose missing in much contemporary poetry." When recounting episodes from family history, he often shows the close bonds between them and the larger world of public history: "Since I am a war baby myself, since I quite literally would not have been born if the Japanese had not crippled my father's ship off Iwo Jima, sending him back to San Francisco where he met my mother at a dance, I have been aware of a debt to history from a very early age" (*Able Muse*, 138).

Although much of his poetry is highly personal, almost in the tradition of the "Confessional School," Mason often stresses the public or communal dimension of poetry. This attitude lay behind his acceptance of the role of Poet Laureate of Colorado. Talking about the classical origins of the word *laureate*, he stated: "When you think of the ancients, you realize their poets had a strong relationship to community. Sappho may have spoken to a school of young women. Aeschylus and Sophocles fought in the wars before earning their bays. The plays of Aeschylus are essentially communal things—about the city, the community and the bringing of justice to mankind. Those of Sophocles are often about notions of piety in relation to the secular city" (*Connotation Press* interview). Mason thus counters prevailing notions of the poet as essentially a rebel or outsider; such notions can be traced back to the Romantics and were subsequently passed from "Baudelaire and Rimbaud to a generation like the Midcentury American poets, so many of whom were mentally ill or suicidal, to the Beats, despite the fact that Ginsberg became a millionaire who pontificated on talk shows" (*Connotation Press* interview).

Naturally, he was aware of the risks involved in becoming an "official poet," and in the same interview he ironically cites "Robert Burns's scathing greeting to King George III in 'A Dream.'" There are, of course, any number of examples of uninspired and uninspiring poet laureates, from Colley Cibber to Robert Southey, and the role is one that has been mocked in memorable fashion by numerous poets, from Byron to Tony Harrison. But Mason chose to take his duties as laureate seriously, imposing on himself the task of visiting every county in the state and promoting poetry in all venues possible, from prisons to schools to county halls and hospitals. He also accepted the duty of writing poems in response to tragic events in the state, such as the disastrous Waldo Canyon fire and the Aurora cinema killings.

As Mason's remarks on the origins of the word *laureate* indicate, Greece has played a major role in his formation as a poet—and in the formation of his ideas on poetry. The decision to travel to Greece was taken for reasons that were entirely personal. It served as a kind of break in his life, after the tragic death of his brother in a climbing accident; the original plan had been to travel to Scotland, where "I would write and Jonna would—what? What would she do? That was the rub. She saw herself in this frozen croft where I would soak in Celtic atmosphere, hammering out poems and stories, and she, perhaps, would knit" (*News from the Village*, 14). Instead, the couple opted for a warm country. "The Scottish novel became the Greek novel. I changed the names."

The novel never materialized, but the yearlong stay in the Mani region of Greece proved crucial for a number of reasons. One was the contact he established with the legendary English writer Patrick Leigh Fermor, who lived close to the young American couple and became a lifelong friend of Mason. He could be said to have served as a role model, exemplifying the ideal of the writer as "a man of the world in the very best sense" (64), whose writings reveal both scholarship and the authority of lived experience. Mason has written memorable pages on Leigh Fermor, celebrating what he calls the "transformative powers" of his books: "To call them travel books is far too limiting. They are works of imagination, a form of poetry." Just as crucially, the time spent in Greece opened Mason's eyes to other ways of living, to "a different kind of rootedness," as Andrew Frisardi expresses it. "Greece in Mason's poems is both Epicurean and Homeric; it is an image of intense sensual presence and unreflective vitality—part of his drive to 'feel more alive in [his] own skin,' as he puts it in *Ludlow*." And, of course, Greece represents 3,000 years of poetic tradition.

All these factors, combined with the newly awakened sense of the importance of understanding things in their political and historic context, helped to shape Mason as a poet. They partly explain the topic he chose for his PhD dissertation some six years after his return to America: the long poems of W. H. Auden. Despite the famous dictum in his elegy for W. B. Yeats, "Poetry makes nothing happen," few poets have reflected more fruitfully on the social role of poetry than Auden. Mason's dissertation, written under the supervision of Anthony Hecht and Daniel Albright, analyzes the long poems Auden embarked on in the second half of his career. Although ranging widely in form, content, and tone, these longer works all show Auden attempting to overcome what he saw as the division of the poet from the society for which he wrote, a division that had its roots in the Romantic age, when poets, to use Auden's own words, "became introspective, obscure, and highbrow" (preface to *The Oxford Book of Light Verse*). Of course, as Auden was all too aware, this was an accusation that could have been leveled against himself in the earlier part of his career.

Mason's dissertation is an extremely fascinating document. Although he has never published it, he has clearly drawn on his studies in some of his later essays on the poet. The dissertation throws interesting light on how Mason came to form his own views of the communal role of the poet:

For Auden the notion of an ivory tower is anathema, and so is the notion of an artist martyred by a misunderstanding public. Art that insists on its superior isolation denies the humanity, the doubleness, of the artist. It could well be said with James Longenbach that a good many modernist poets, particularly Pound and Yeats, had developed "an unbearably inflated Romantic conception of the poet's social function." (44)

Mason acknowledges that it would be oversimplistic to consider Auden purely as a public poet, ignoring the private dimensions of his work; as he remarks, Auden points to both Dryden, "primarily a public poet," and Catullus, "an intimately private one," as his mentors, and these "two figures reflect a tension within Auden's own work" (56). But the general trend of the argument in the dissertation is to emphasize Auden's more communal role; in a footnote, Mason approvingly refers to Mendelson's preface to the *Selected Poems*, in which Mendelson "demonstrates that Auden's public program increasingly stresses communication, a public stance for the poet, that is not based upon the centrality of his or her private world or feeling" (123).

It was not only the subject matter of the thesis that played a major role in forming Mason as a poet, but also the senior poet who codirected the dissertation, Anthony Hecht. Mason had deliberately chosen the University of Rochester for his graduate studies because he wanted to be taught by Hecht. He had first met him in the late 1970s, while he was working as a gardener in Rochester. This initial encounter amounted to no more than a handshake after attending a reading given by Hecht, but when he returned to Rochester from Greece, emboldened by his encounters with Leigh Fermor and other writers, he plucked up courage to ask Hecht for another meeting, which resulted in an hour-long conversation about books at the senior poet's house.

Even though Hecht left the university while Mason was there to take up a post at Georgetown University, he continued to codirect the dissertation by mail. Hecht was one of many poets of his generation to have been directly and profoundly influenced by Auden, as can be seen in his book-length study of the poet (in which he makes generous acknowledgment of Mason's help), and he was able to transmit to Mason a sense of almost direct contact with Auden.

Reading Mason's essay on Hecht as a war poet in *Two Minds of a Western Poet*, one can see why he felt so drawn to the older poet. Despite all the differences in their backgrounds and temperaments, there were some crucial things that they shared. Hecht himself seems to have been aware of this, as Mason suggests: "Not given to effusive emotions with people he barely knew, he told me I reminded him of men he had known on the G.I. Bill after the war. My eager pursuit of literary knowledge could not be divorced from a broader experience of struggle in life" (79). It was not until Mason sat down to write his essay on Hecht's war poetry that he "realized [Hecht] was also touching on aspects of himself" (79). While fully aware of the vast difference between the kinds of experience the two poets had had before embarking on their literary careers ("I had seen extremes of human behavior and some violence, but nothing like the mechanized slaughter Tony witnessed in the war," 80), Mason sees their predilection for "the formalities of art" as stemming from similar impulses. He expresses this notion with memorable and penetrating simplicity: "Life without the shaping impulse can be hard for some of us to bear" (80).

Hecht's poetry serves as a brilliant refutation of the prevailing twentieth- and twenty-first-century notion that art in a chaotic age needs itself to be chaotic. Few poets have witnessed so directly the horrors of warfare as did Hecht, who testified that, after his experiences in participating in the liberation of the concentration camp of Flossenburg, "for years after I would wake shrieking" (Hoy, 24); however, his poetry—even that which deals directly with the topic of the Holocaust—is elaborately formal and patterned. This deliberate artistic choice is perhaps best illuminated by an observation in Hecht's book *On the Laws of the Poetic Art:*

What both poems and funerals do is to give formality—even a ceremonious and traditional formality—to what otherwise would be unmediated feeling: in the case of funerals the lamentations of raw grief, and the perfunctory dumping of a body in the ground. Raw grief is terrible and undeniable emotion; it lies beyond criticism. But it also lies beyond art. And to the degree that a poem wants to express grief, it must make some concessions to formality. (143)

There is no doubt that this is a viewpoint with which Mason sympathizes. The great majority of his poetry is in form, even if rarely in the highly elaborate stanza forms that Hecht chose for some of his greatest poems. As Frisardi has put it, "He doesn't dazzle with technical flamboyance—his language is a steady surface, energetic as all poetry must be, but contained. Like his mentor Robert Frost, Mason's style is characterized by artful plainness; he brings meter to life with American speech rhythms." In his essay "The Poetry of Life and the Life of Poetry," Mason declares, "Our greatest pleasures often derive from form— the feeling of connection, completion, touch. It seems that the mind naturally rejects formlessness" (19).

It is no surprise, therefore, that Mason has come to be identified closely with the New Formalist movement, even though he has declared his dissatisfaction with the term: "Maybe it's time to let the term wither away. As it happens, I have always disparaged it in private and in print, largely because I mistrust claims of novelty and believe that formalist designs are insufficient markers of any art"

(*Two Minds*, 134). There may be something a little disin-
genuous in this statement, given the fact that he coedited
Rebel Angels, an anthology with the subtitle *25 Poets of the
New Formalism*. It is probably unfair to make too much
of this question, however, since Mason has never been a
narrow-minded polemicist in the so-called Poetry Wars.
Referring to a lighthearted comment he had made on the
term "expansive poetry" ("the title sounded like a balloon
about to burst"), he declared, "What underlay my comment was partly an anxiety about being too easily pegged
as any sort of poet. While it is true that I have encountered
editors hostile to rhyme and meter—and even one who
advised me to avoid rich sound effects like alliteration—it
is also true that I wanted to be free to attempt any poetic form available, from free verse to the verse novel" (*Two
Minds*, 135).

He stated that his model in formal terms "was a protean figure like Auden," adding that he "wanted an earthier
sense of peoples' lives in what I wrote" (*Two Minds*, 135).
As he has declared, "Auden was actually weak in narrative and dramatic poems" and therefore could not serve
as a model for this side of his art. The major influence on
his narrative poetry, as Frisardi points out, is undoubtedly Robert Frost, as earthy a poet as one could hope for.
Like Frost, Mason relies principally on iambic measures
for his narratives and usually endeavors to create the impression of a speaking voice. Apart from his novel-length
work *Ludlow*, his narratives have mainly taken the form of

dramatic monologues, sometimes intertwining two such monologues, as in "The Country I Remember." Although Mason's speakers have their own distinctive voices, it is easy to see that he is writing in the tradition of such striking verse tales as "A Servant to Servants" or "The Witch of Coös."

Mason has become one of the strongest voices in support of the revival—or perhaps more aptly the pursuance—of the tradition of narrative poetry. He has written numerous essays on the vitality of contemporary verse narrative, pointing out the advantages that verse offers for the recounting of forceful tales, showing how one "can hear the adjustments of dramatic voice in relation to the line, almost a musical interplay in which the entire form of a completed story becomes audible" (*Poetry of Life*, 181). Dramatic voice also means that the poet can escape the confines of his or her own ego, which can be greatly enriching: "I also think poets can learn the power of empathy from fiction writers. Poets can write about a bigger world if they inhabit other people's skin for a while" ("Dramatic Voice," Eratosphere). Elsewhere he has declared that "poets who tell stories admit that we are in this together, that individual talent is not enough. Our anger and grief can be shared" (*Two Minds*, 41). This is something that probably became even more important to him during his years as poet laureate.

Once again, we return to the notion of poetry as a communal art. Given Mason's experiences in the film world, it is perhaps not surprising that he has also sought analogies with cinema, perhaps the most communal art form of the present day, for some of the effects that are possible in narrative verse. In the afterword to *Ludlow*, Mason declares, "verse is often more cinematic than prose in its rhythm and images, its narrative economy" (228). He points by way of example to the old Scottish ballads, where "a simple stanza allows the poet to reject reams of exposition." Elsewhere he has quoted Matthew Hodgart, the editor of *The Faber Book of Ballads*, who referred to the conventions of ballad as storytelling in "sharp flashes." The ballad requires that the reader or auditor's imagination fills in the gaps; this is possible because of a shared understanding of the conventions of the form.

The notion of something shared underlies all of Mason's work. Poetry may be written in solitude, but it is written with the aim of reaching out to other people. He concludes perhaps his most important essay, "The Poetry of Life and the Life of Poetry" (also the title of the book in which it is contained), by telling a story about his mother. He had never thought of her as a poetry reader, and yet when she needed to communicate to him her feelings about his father ("She wanted me to know that she still loved my father, despite all the hell they put each other through"), she did so by directing his attention to a poem by Yeats ("A Deep-Sworn Vow"). Reflecting on this, Mason concludes his essay with these words:

Yeats's voice speaks across time. It is specific to his life, his loves and prejudices. Yet it becomes one of our voices too, the imagination pressing back against the pressure of reality. The poetry of life and the life of poetry mean that reality alone is no place to live. (31–32)

We learn a good deal about Mason's life through his poetry: we learn of his family life and troubles, his travels, his loves, and his losses, but we never have the impression of being buttonholed by a man who is self-centered or egoistical. Partly this is because we are convinced of the numerous ways in which the life he recounts is connected to other lives, to places and to historical events. But it is mainly because we always sense how closely what he recounts is related to ourselves. As with all major poets, his voice becomes our own.

CHAPTER 2

Biography

David Mason was born in 1954 in Bellingham, Washington, the second of three sons of professional parents. His father had started out as a pediatrician and then become a psychiatrist, while his mother was a professor of psychology at Western Washington University. Mason spent his childhood in Washington State, paying frequent visits to Colorado to visit his paternal relatives. The very different landscapes and climates of the two states were to inform his poetry from the start. His parents separated in 1966 and divorced in 1969.

Mason attended Colorado College between 1973 and 1974 and then dropped out to work on crab boats in Dutch Harbor, Alaska. Between January and July 1975, he spent seven months on the road in Europe, traveling through Britain, France, Ireland, and Spain. He returned to America in the summer of 1975 and reenrolled at Colorado College in the autumn, graduating with a BA in English in 1978. During his undergraduate studies, he met

Jonatha Heinrich, whom he married in April 1978. After graduating, he worked as a gardener and caretaker in Irondequoit (a suburb of Rochester, his wife's hometown). His younger brother, Don, was a photography student at the Rochester Institute of Technology at the time.

On August 26, 1979, he received a nighttime telephone call from his stepfather, Art, telling him that his elder brother, Doug, had died while climbing Mount Shuksan (near Bellingham) with Don. This event was to be a major trauma for the whole family and severely aggravated his mother's alcoholism. For Mason, it was a kind of tragic watershed in his life, and he was to return to it over and over again in his poetry.

In August 1980, determined to make a break with things, Mason and Jonna set off for Greece, where he intended to write a novel. They settled in Kardamyli, in the Mani region, near the house of the English writer Patrick Leigh Fermor, in Kalamitsi Bay. They remained in Greece until November 1981, when Mason was offered a screenwriting job, adapting the novel he had written about his Alaskan experiences. This yearlong stay in Greece established a bond with the country that remains strong to the present day, even though he was not to return to the country for another sixteen years. While working on the film script (never to be produced, just as the novel was never published), Mason stayed in Los Angeles with his great-aunt, Mary Hertz, who told him stories of her grandfather during the Civil War, which would later feed into his narrative poem "The Country I Remember."

In 1984, Mason entered graduate school at the University of Rochester, wishing to study with the poet Anthony Hecht. He obtained an MA degree in 1986 and a PhD in 1989, with a dissertation on the long poems of W. H. Auden, supervised by Hecht (who had moved to Georgetown University in 1985 but continued to follow Mason's work by correspondence) and Daniel Albright.

In 1987, David Mason and Jonna divorced, and on October 16, 1988, he married Anne Lennox, a photographer, daughter of Scottish immigrants. Between 1989 and 1998, he taught at Moorhead State University in Minnesota (he was named Minnesota Outstanding Professor of the Year in 1994). He published his first book of poetry, *The Buried Houses*, in 1991. It was followed by *The Country I Remember* in 1996.

In the same year he coedited, with Mark Jarman, *Rebel Angels*, a key anthology in the New Formalist movement. It was his first editorial experience; over the next decade, he was to work on a number of important anthologies, including various editions of *Western Wind* (at first together with John Frederick Nims) and *Twentieth Century American Poetry* (with Dana Gioia and Meg Schoerke). In addition, at the end of the 1980s, he began to work as a regular reviewer and essay writer for a number of publications, in particular the *Hudson Review*.

In the spring semester of 1997, he finally made his way

back to Greece on a Fulbright fellowship. It was to be the first of many returns to the country, where he established a network of good friends. This connection with Greece has also led to numerous translations of works by major poets, such as Cavafy, Chouliaras, Palamas, Ritsos, and Seferis.

In 1998, he returned to Colorado College as an assistant professor, becoming a full professor in 2008. In 2000, he published a book of essays, *The Poetry of Life and the Life of Poetry*, and his third book of poems, *Arrivals*, in 2004. His family life, meanwhile, was troubled by his father's descent into Alzheimer disease at the end of the 1990s; he died in 2003. Toward the end of her life, Mason's mother-in-law, who was also suffering from Alzheimer disease, moved in with him and Annie. She lived with them for six years, dying in 2004.

In 2007, Mason published his verse novel, *Ludlow*, centered on a massacre that occurred during labor disputes in the Colorado coal fields at the beginning of the twentieth century. It was his most ambitious narrative poem to date. Three years later, he published his account of his Greek travels and friendships, *News from the Village* (2010). He was appointed Poet Laureate of Colorado in the same year, a four-year post. His second book of essays, *Two Minds of a Western Poet*, came out in 2011.

In July 2011, his mother died, while Mason was traveling in Great Britain with Chrissy Allinson, known to the literary world as the Australian poet Cally Conan-Davies. She became his third wife in 2012. The couple bought a house in Oregon, so for a while Mason divided his time between Colorado, where he had rented a cabin after the separation from Annie, and Oregon. The idea was that when he retired from university teaching, they would settle by the sea, and he would devote himself to writing full time.

Sea Salt: Poems for a Decade was published in 2014, and his third collection of essays, *Voices, Places*, came out in 2018. A new field opened for him in the second decade of the century, as he became closely involved with the world of opera. He collaborated with the composer Lori Laitman on various projects, including an opera based on *The Scarlet Letter* (the libretto was published in 2012 as *The Scarlet Libretto*, and the opera was premiered in 2016), an oratorio about children in the concentration camp of Terezin, and an operatic version of *Ludlow*. He has also written libretti for two operas with the composer Tom Cipullo, *After Life* and *The Parting*, which premiered in 2015 and 2019, respectively.

In 2017, the Masons spent the summer holidays in Australia (winter there, of course) and began to look for a house in Tasmania, having changed their minds about retirement in Oregon. As the Tasmanian market was heating up, they realized that if they were to be able to afford a decent home, they would have to move quickly. They put the Oregon house on the market in November and sold it in December. In January 2018, after the formal closing on the house sale, Chrissy flew to Tasmania and put in an offer on a house south of Hobart, which they had seen online. They formally acquired the house and five acres of land in February 2018. Mason arrived in May to start a sabbatical year in Australia and to begin his immigration process. When he returned to the United States in September 2019, he knew it was for his final year of teaching. The college granted him early retirement, which consisted of three years of half salary as he eased out. The COVID-19 pandemic hit in March 2020, and the college went to online teaching, so he booked a flight home—which is to say, Tasmania—and arrived in late March 2020. He and Chrissy have lived there ever since.

CHAPTER 3

Buried Houses

Mason's first collection, *Buried Houses*, appeared in 1991 (two chapbooks—*Blackened Peaches* and *Small Elegies*—had appeared in 1989 and 1990, respectively) and won the Nicholas Roerich Poetry Prize for that year. It is divided into three untitled sections, each one containing a mixture of lyrics and narratives, both autobiographical and fictional. A wide range of forms are adopted throughout the book, although blank verse seems to prevail; there are also a number of poems in quatrains and cinquains. Three longish narratives in blank verse are to be found in the first two sections. The narratives have generally attracted the most attention and perhaps give the clearest indication of the way Mason's career would develop. But despite some uneven poems (and some metrical uncertainties, as Mason himself has acknowledged), the book demonstrates the range of his concerns and his determination to savor all the possibilities offered by English verse.

If one were to seek distinguishing features in each of

the various sections, one might be tempted to point to the different geographical settings, with Europe dominating in the first, the western states of Washington and Colorado in the second, while the third ranges across America and Scotland. Such distinctions are by no means rigid, however, and the temptation to draw them is perhaps mainly indicative of the extreme importance of location in Mason's work.

The first section contains a few anomalous poems, suggesting that Mason is still seeking his voice. This category includes, for example, two literary works; the pantoum "**Gusev**," based on a short story by Chekhov; and "**Explorations**," based on a line from a poem by Hart Crane. "**The Feast of the Rose Garlands**," which explores the aesthetic obsessions of the emperor Rudolf II, offers a kind of historical and artistic meditation that does not have many parallels in Mason's later work, although the theme of desire and possession is one he will frequently examine.

A key poem in the section is the elegy for Bruce Chatwin, already referred to in the opening chapter. Mason would write more extensively of Chatwin, whom he had met in Greece, in later prose, but this poem already indicates what it was in the writer's life and works that fascinated him. Using a rueful first-person plural, Mason contrasts the life of "the ones who settle and destroy, / build and regret, wishing we could leave it" with that of the restless Chatwin, able to "sling the moment's household on [his] back / looking ahead at open roads and fields / no crows darken ..." As Mason's later essays would indicate, however, there was a paradoxical side to Chatwin's character; despite presenting himself as a free traveler who had renounced the desire for possessions, he remained to the end an obsessive collector of curios and objects. Mason's poem hints at this paradox in its title, "**The Thing Worth Saving.**" With its reference to "the hide of mylodon" that allegedly sparked Chatwin's fascination with Patagonia, the subject of his first travel book, Mason's poem points to the fact that a travel writer, even while presenting an image of himself as unencumbered and free, is always concerned to "save" things.

The title could indeed be applied to the whole book. It is a book about "things worth saving," in memory if not in fact. In this sense, Rudolf II's obsession with his Dürer painting is not so untypical a figure in the book. In the same section, we encounter the old Brit at his "usual waterfront café" in Greece, determined to preserve his memories of the war and resenting the changes imposed by the new invasion of "German youth." The most moving poems of the book, in the second section, show the poet himself engaged in keeping the memories of his brother and their shared childhood alive. In the final section, the poem "**Disclosure**" (which Mason would also include in his prose memoir, *News from the Village*), about the breakup of his first marriage, states: "It's strange what we can make ourselves believe. / Memory saves; recrimination uses / every twisted syllable of the past." The poem

attempts a less embittered use of those things preserved by memory, declaring categorically, "I say our marriage was a gentle thing," and proving this was so by pointing to the little objects preserved from the past that testify to a shared gentleness: "gifts / collected long ago, drawings of a house / we lived in, letters from friends we haven't told […] a book I signed, a scarf you knitted …"

The book celebrates the genuineness of such things and their irreplaceability. Indeed, in the poem that closes the first section, "**Recipe**," the poet takes some delight in acknowledging the limitations of poetry in evoking such things as the pleasures of the table. Although the poet does his best to conjure the dishes created by his friend—"Collops of chicken sauted in olive oil […] Onions, deftly chopped, and peeled tomatoes / bubble in oil with olives from Kalamata"—and anticipates the added pleasure of "garnish[ing] conversation with a line from Frost / or Yeats' palpable distillations"—he recognizes in the final lines that his friend's provision is one that "no one can publish or repeat."

Despite this rueful (but also delighted) admission of the limitations of poetry, Mason's poetry is very much connected with the world of things and with the things of this world, and it is committed to celebrating their concrete existence. As already hinted, one way in which he does this is by paying close attention to geographical settings, to natural features of landscapes, and to climatic conditions. "Recipe," while clearly set indoors, brings to a close a series of poems that evoke the Mediterranean world. Three of them are written in the first person, but only one of the speakers, the voice in "**The Bone House**," seems identifiable with the poet himself. "**The Old Brit**" gives us the angry grumbling of a veteran from the Second World War, unable to reconcile himself with the fact that the Germans have returned to Greece, this time as holidaymakers; his wartime reminiscences powerfully evoke the heat and grit of desert warfare, still brought to him "when the simoom blows from Libya." "The Bone House," written in long-lined free-verse quatrains, also evokes an arid world, where only the cicadas seem alive, scraping the air "like mad inheritors." "**The Nightingales of Andritsena**," the longest of these poems, is the monologue of a middle-aged American woman tour guide and uses the Greek background to set off the speaker's sad and lonely longings; I will discuss this poem more extensively toward the end of this chapter.

The opening poem of the book's second section, "**What Is It There?**," seems deliberately placed to provide as strong a contrast as possible with the concluding poems of the previous section. From the opening lines, describing "an atmosphere / laden with water," we are taken into a land of ice, of rivers "green with glacial silt," of "mist exhalations" and dampness. The sounds of this landscape are the "muffled roar / as water falls and ice breaks free" and "the river's clatter." The questioning title of the poem indicates the problem of defining anything in this hazy world of "memories or myths." Sight is baffled both by the mist and by the woods that "no eye can penetrate," and sounds are rendered indistinct by the "slow descent of clouds." But at the end of the poem, we get the disturbing intrusion of a mother's scream "for her lost son," heralding the theme of loss, which will dominate the whole section.

The second poem, **"Versions of Ecotopia,"** recalls in its title Ernest Callenbach's 1974 novel, set in a futuristic state, consisting of Northern California, Oregon, and Washington. From the opening stanza, Mason's poem creates a picture of the land where he grew up as a place that is both desirable and somewhat fantastic, perhaps even dreamlike:

> God help the land that is unlucky enough
> to be popular, where everyone wants the view
> of islands like loaves and fishes in the west,
> the seiner placed just right in the composition,
> and rain is gentle as a Japanese scroll.

As the title suggests, Mason's eye is also on environmental issues ("As murdered buffalo disturb our dreaming plains ..."). Even while describing some of the less desirable recent developments ("a bit of Phoenix by the oyster beds, / a Trumpish tower downtown ..."), he takes advantage of the oneiric atmosphere he has created to evoke the specter of the mythical Paul Bunyan at the end of the poem: "At night the plaid giant rattles his axe / and growls in Swedish, up to his neck in muck, / where the tall, unbarbered forest used to be." The final stanza takes us back to the beginning of the poem, maintaining the imagery of marine and pluvial dampness:

> You find yourself in unexpected traffic,
> pressed in a narrow shoal of weeping lights,
> looking through the rain for an exit sign,
> and thinking of an old scroll you once saw
> rubbed to nothing by a billion loving hands.

We remain in this western coastal landscape in the next poem, "**In the Islands**," which is the first of a number of poems devoted to childhood reminiscences. It describes a seaside holiday under the distracted attention of a certain Mrs. Pocket, "who sat against a log, / engrossed in a paperback…" The first four stanzas seem to evoke an idyllic protected world; however, there are indications that not all is as innocent and secure as it might first appear. There is the disturbing detail of the power of the sea, which leaves the children "appalled" at "how far the kelp had been dragged up, / left like silage from a great combine." The beach itself is their playground because the "inland world" where the crows hawk is "dense and inaccessible." The children engage in the game of "subjugat[ing] neighborhoods of tiny crabs / who scampered from the light," and there is the suggestion that the children themselves are living in as illusory a state of safety as the crabs beneath their rocks. In the fourth stanza, the poet switches to the first-person singular, describing how he "crawled inside a rack of driftwood, / pretending it was home." As already mentioned, this is a subtle and telling image of false security.

In the opening lines of the next stanza, the poet disconcertingly shifts temporal perspective: "By now, insinuating tides have tugged it apart. / Mrs. Pocket finished her book, and sometime later / died of cancer." The very next poem in the book, "**The Buried Houses**," uses the same strategy, on a vaster scale, to even more unsettling effect. This time, the poem is openly about the breakup of the family ("We were a family then …"), and Mason uses the archaeological digging of an ancient village on the coast "as a correlative for lost family unity" (Hix, 210). The first details of the discovery are disturbing: "They found a wooden dorsal sequinned with otter teeth, / the terrifying masks that would have called to spirits / whose longhouses lay two hundred fathoms deep." As they reconstruct this lost world, however, its details become less disconcerting, "a buried world / whose dailiness was well-suited to this coast." By the end of the poem, it is the world of the present day that is more mysterious and disconcerting: "Much is known by now about the buried houses, / less about the people who uncovered them."

The next poem is titled "**A Textbook of Navigation and Nautical Astronomy**." The book referred to in the title, found among the author's own poetry books, belonged to his father, and the poet broods on it in an effort to get closer to his father and his wartime experiences. He wonders whether "his skill at navigating saved him" after he left the "affectionate strangers / who shared his house." The poem makes constant use of the language of navigational precision, with the stars offering clear reference points; however, it ends with an image of dark uncertainty and the resigned words: "No one can tell you what to see."

The five poems that follow are all devoted to the most traumatic event in Mason's life, the death of his elder brother, Douglas, at the age of 28, in a climbing accident on Mount Shuksan near Bellingham, on August 26, 1979. Mason himself was working as a gardener and caretaker in a suburb of Rochester when he received the late-night phone call from his stepfather. He approaches this devastating subject first through Greek mythology and through dream, in a poem titled "**At the Graves of Castor and Pollux**," and then directly through a poem in two sections titled "**Small Elegies**." In the first section, he speaks in his own voice, describing his visit to the mortician's and the sight of his brother, down to the detail of "the blood on one of his motionless fingers, / filmed with dirt from the mountain that he climbed." In the second section, he speaks in the voice of his younger brother, who had been climbing with Doug and had witnessed the fatal fall. Both poems are painstakingly clear, describing the sights and sensations of the tragic events with powerful directness. There is no recourse to figurative language; however, the last two lines of the second section—"My hands still felt, from earlier that day, / the tension of my brother's weight on the rope"—while testifying to a direct physical sensation, also preannounce the burden of grief that will continue to weigh down on the poet for years to come.

The next two poems in the sequence evoke the pleasures and pains of mountain-climbing. When we read the lines "Otherwise this sun-scrubbed clarity / stabbing off the ice" in "**The Mountain Climber**," we almost have the sensation that we are reading the aesthetic credo that lies behind the poem itself. With its short-lined quatrains, it seems to be seeking a kind of pared-down essentiality in its diction and form—like the glacier, which we are told is "peeling the mountain down." While the poem begins with the evocation of upward movement, the subsequent image of the glacier, "falling to its own return," ominously heralds the fall of the body, which takes place over a crucially placed enjambment between two stanzas: "The body is constantly // to fall." The second of these two mountain-climbing poems describes the two surviving brothers doing a climb in Colorado, almost in tribute to their elder brother. The title itself, "**Dry Granite**," indicates the difference in climate and geology from the scene of Doug's fall. We have the sense that the climb, which seems more painful than pleasurable, is a kind of necessary ritual, enabling the mind to achieve something like the "absolute clarity" of the air and water. Although the body remains "bent and trembling" in the "briared jam-crack" of the rock, there is something cleansing in the quiet air and motionless granite; the poem ends on this note of freshened clarity: "The water curving below / washes stones in the sunlight."

The final poem to deal directly with the death, "**An Absence**," takes us away from the mountains of the West to the poet's new home in the East, "another state / with hills for mountains and less rain." The only one in the sequence to rhyme, the poem concludes with quiet words that sound ritualistic and almost prayerlike:

> I've grown by distances, and lost
> that place where I could visit you.
> Though nothing's written on your stone,
> I hope you never feel alone.
> I hope it feels like rest.

The poem that follows acts like a kind of coda to the sequence, declaring itself in the title to be unabashedly a "**Journal and Prayer**." The voice is that of a mother with alcohol problems, one of whose sons "died in mountains— oh, six years ago." She is now brooding on her lonely life, in a study "with a view / of islands where my children used to play." She talks of a priest, Father Clark, who has spent time in jail in China and who is capable of talking "lightly" of his imprisonment in a windowless cell. The word "light," in its various meanings, returns like a steady refrain, almost as if to reproach her choice of staying in her room "with shades drawn tight." Her world consists now of absences and losses, symbolized by the imagery of empty chairs and echoes, and of a drained wading pool "where now light rain / pasted leaves to cement." The final lines are a prayer, in which "for no reason, and without

confirmed belief" she asks that her loss be somehow made fruitful; the word "lighten" suggests a plea to be at once freed from the burden of her grief and drawn forth from the gloom of her shadowy spaces:

> All I have lost is fed into these trees;
> lighten me, Lord, with your green presence.

After another elegy, this time for a friend, the book's second section concludes with three longer poems, two of them fictional narratives and one a portrait of an old family friend. As the narratives have been generally recognized as the book's most important works, I will leave them to the end of this discussion.

The third section contains the customary mixture of narrative poems and meditative lyrics. The latter seem mainly personal: the first, **"Disclosure"** (mentioned above), delicately treats the breakup of the poet's first marriage, and several of the other poems apparently draw on episodes from the courtship of his second wife. As always, there is a good deal of geographical movement, as the poet compares their "childhoods back / to back, a continent between" (**"Summer Nights"**) and then goes back even further, to his wife's infancy in Scotland (**"A Map of Scotland"**). One poem, **"Letter from New York,"** moves rather confusingly from New York to Colorado and back again. The image of the sunlit, snow-covered high plains from a speeding car and subsequently from a plane ("the snow / endlessly unbroken") provides a suggestive correlative for the state of bemusement that the poem evokes. The fictional narrative poem "**The Next Place**" is also a poem of movement, describing the travels of a couple of hucksters around Colorado. After all this ceaseless movement, the book ends with the image of swallows: "But I assume they know / what it's like to be lost in endless circles / and, suddenly weightless, sense which way to fly."

In general, critics have agreed that the most important poems in the book are the narratives. All four of them are in the first person; indeed, given the mingling of fiction and personal recollection in the book, the reader might understandably read "Spooning," the first narrative in the second section, as a story about Mason's childhood; however, a moment's Googling will bring to light the fact that the film star mentioned in the narrative, Lydia Truman Gates, exists only in this poem. The other poems, having female or noncontemporary speakers, immediately declare themselves as fictional works, although "Blackened Peaches," as Mason himself has declared, is in the voice of an old family friend. With the exception of "The Next Place," which is written in loose tetrameter lines, the poems are in blank verse.

The first of these narratives, "**The Nightingales of Andritsena**," is a monologue by Mrs. Finn, a "sadly middle-aged" divorcée who works as a translator and tour guide for American students in Greece. She observes with a mixture of melancholy and envy the easy, thoughtless love of her young charges. We gradually pick up details of her past: the philandering husband who left her, her children in America, and most crucially, her father's "suicide / in Chicago in 1939," the last lines of the poem. At the heart of the poem is the moment when she and a young couple go out to listen to the famous nightingales of the town, "capable of twelve distinctive melodies." Mrs. Finn quotes to herself the refrain from Seferis's poem, "Helen": "*The nightingales won't let you sleep in Platres.*" She allows herself to be "caught up by, of all things, a rhythm"—the repeated words "Won't let you sleep, won't let you sleep."

Mason has written extensively on Seferis, clearly a favorite poet. In *News from the Village*, he reports an occasion when a group of Greek friends, driving in search of a restaurant on Long Island, started singing Theodorakis's version of Seferis's "Epiphany, 1937" and Mason felt that he "was hearing the pure poetry of exile" (*News*, 143). In an essay in *Two Minds*, Mason declares: "Some poets are born of language, others are born of language and place, a sort of mutual saturation of word and experience. Seferis is the latter kind of poet" (*Two Minds*, 155). And so, of course, is Mason himself. Mrs. Finn's evocation of this figure, who was paradoxically a poet of both exile and place, is not a casual one.

But the key scene—"the epiphany of Mrs. Finn," as she puts it, with rueful irony—is actually an anticlimax: "For me it had all gone flat [...] / [...] I saw how we transformed it in our minds / to what we had expected it to be." It is essentially a moment that underlines her separateness;

she is excluded from the "evening's mood" that envelopes the two young people and finds herself dismissing it as "a shell / of words—of empty, captivating words." The refrain from Seferis's poem returns, and we recall that the poem it comes from, "Helen," depicts the bitter feelings of those involved in pointless suffering.[1] It is at this point that she reveals the traumatic tragedy that overwhelmed her life in childhood.

"**Spooning**," the second of these narratives, announces in the old-fashioned slang of its title that it tells a story of former times. The narrator recounts the story of how, as a child, he was told by his grandfather that he had once been caught "spooning" with Lydia Truman Gates. The child has no idea what the word means, nor who Lydia Truman Gates is; however, shortly afterward, the film star from the days of silent movies comes back to the town to celebrate the renovation of the old movie theatre. The narrator and his brother take the opportunity to approach the star, and they discover that she really does remember their grandfather; she says that she "knew he'd never get out of this town," which, of course, has proved true.

It is a poem about relations between different generations and about the discovery of unexpected dimensions to people. We are told at the opening of the poem that after his grandfather's death, the narrator helped his mother

1. The epigraph to Seferis's poem comes from Euripides's play *Helen*, in which it is revealed that Helen, over whom the Trojan war was fought, was nothing but a phantom.

"sell his furniture: / the old chair he did his sitting on, / the kitchen things." The curious description of the chair (later, the narrator describes his grandfather as apparently talking more "to his chair's abrasions on the floor") suggests a confined life; he had once owned a car and "got as far as Spokane's desert" but then spent the rest of his life as a shopkeeper in the small town. His only escape consisted in talking, but purely to the grandchildren, the intermediate generation apparently dismissing his tales as daydreams. The story shows the children discovering the truth of the most surprising of his tales and at the same time gaining a sense of the past—even against the will of their parents:

> Our mother said we had better things to spend
> our money on than some old movie house,
> though she remembered how it used to look.
> She said that people living in the past
> wouldn't amount to much.

Even as she dismisses the devotion to the past, the qualifying phrase ("though she remembered how it used to look …") indicates how impossible it is to shake off memories. The climax of the story is, of course, the arrival of the great film star. The contrast between the "frail old woman assisted by two men" and the flickering vision of the actress who "arose in veils, / in something gossamer / astonishing even in 1965" is neatly done. The story does not unequivocally restore the child's faith in his grandfather; he is left upset by the actress's quip, "Is he still alive? / Too scared to come downtown and say hello?" The final impression on the child, bewildered by the popping flash-bulbs, seems to be one of bemusement, so that he is left apparently questioning the reality of the actress—and, by implication, perhaps that of the adult world as a whole:

> I thought of her decaying on a screen,
> her ribs folding like a silk umbrella's rods,
> while all the men who gathered around her
> clutched at the remnants of her empty dress.

The last of the blank-verse narratives, **"Blackened Peaches,"** is generally recognized as the finest poem in the book, even though Mason himself has acknowledged weaknesses in the meter. The poem comes immediately after a four-sonnet sequence titled **"Long Life,"** which is an affectionate portrait of an elderly neighbor whom Mason knew as "Auntie Wright," as she often used to care for the Mason children when their parents were out working. The four sonnets are essentially a tribute to a great storyteller, whose stories helped to create his sense of the place where he grew up. Mason has said in an interview that "Auntie Wright was simply one of the best storytellers I have ever known in my life, and at every meal I listened, rapt, to her voice" (*Able Muse*, 138). In the second sonnet, he gives two condensed examples of her stories, matching her own skills by deftly weaving the subject matter into the form of his poem.

In the same interview, he says that it is "her voice, slightly adapted, that I used in my first narrative poem, 'Blackened Peaches,' and her voice I have so often heard pacing out the stories in my head" (138–39). In the opening line of the poem—"One fall it was Jim and me living out / to the county"—he establishes the tone and register of this voice; we are overhearing the reminiscences of a natural storyteller. The story may appear to ramble somewhat, jumping back and forth in time, but it is in fact beautifully orchestrated. R. S. Gwynn describes the poem as the best narrative in the book, declaring that "the poet compresses the gist of a novel that might have been written by Willa Cather into three compact sections" (135). The main story is that of the middle-aged Doctor Hale and his never-articulated love for the narrator. Even though apparently favored by the girl's mother ("Halfway through our party Mama left the room"), the doctor is unable to make his proposal—or, perhaps more creditably, he realizes its inappropriateness. He thus loses her to a younger man, Jim.

The narrator begins with the anecdote that gives the poem its title, recounting the "cold / northeasterly" that "nipped the peach trees so the leaves turned black." The story is one of nipped hopes, principally those of the doctor, but also perhaps those of the narrator herself. The doctor's story is told with a mixture of compassion and tenderness by the narrator, combining the viewpoints of herself as an uncomprehending adolescent and as a saddened and possibly wiser widow. Certain gentle gestures, like the repeated action of removing his glasses and rubbing his nose, testify to the doctor's embarrassment and help to create the picture of a sensitive but lonely man. We get just one glimpse of the doctor in another mood, inadvertently seen by the narrator as he chops wood, revealing stronger passions:

> There was Doctor Hale stripped to the waist
> except for his specs and braces, swinging
> that axe as if he were a younger man.
> When he paused to wipe his brow I could see
> he looked angry, tired, or not right with himself;
> he seemed to want to tear those logs apart
> with bare hands.

Gwynn says of this passage that the "easy movement of Mason's blank verse, the clear sense of voice, and the subtlety of the epiphany that reveals both Dr. Hale's emotional frustration and Sally's instinctive physical revulsion to him mark this as a passage that looks ahead to Mason's more ambitious narratives" (135).

But the true emotional peak of the story is more characteristically a moment of embarrassed silence and separation. It comes when the doctor visits her sick husband; as he emerges from the sick chamber, we are told:

> He took his glasses off, rubbed a sore spot
> on the bridge of his nose, gave me a flat look.
> He said, "Jim's been asking for Sally Peaches."
> There we were in the kitchen, six feet apart
> and silent as frost on the windowpanes.

"Sally Peaches" was the affectionate name he had given her when a child and had ceased to use on the occasion her mother had left him alone with her to propose marriage: "You're too big for that. / I promise I won't baby you again." The narrator had let her husband believe that it was her father's name for her, "the one white lie" she ever told him. The doctor dies shortly afterward, his death foretold by the "blackened leaves" outside the house that winter. He returns as a gentle and beneficent ghost during her husband's final illness.

The last of these narratives, **"The Next Place,"** uncharacteristically, is not in iambic pentameter but in loose tetrameter. It is entirely set in Colorado and tells the story of a traveling charlatan healer who picks up a mysterious woman in his travels; we get the sense that he is fascinated by someone who is even more slippery and mysterious than himself. The poem uses the place names of the state to give an idea of the couple's constant and purposeless movement; indeed, their restlessness is similar to that of Chatwin and is made to seem just as attractive:

> For a year or so we've owned the moon,
> I've tipped my hat to pinyon trees,
> she's curtseyed to a fox,
> and when we pass some mining town
> the sooted stares don't bother us.

Although the poem is uncharacteristic in its form, it looks forward in its theme and setting to the extended narrative in his next book, *The Country I Remember*, which also deals with the pioneering days of the West and a sense of restlessness. And, of course, the owners of "the sooted stares" will become the protagonists of his most important narrative, *Ludlow*. Although Mason has declared that *The Buried Houses* contains mainly apprentice work, it gives clear indications of the major poems that will follow. And in the narratives and elegies we can already hear the firm tones of his highly individual voice.

CHAPTER 4

The Country I Remember

Mason's second book, *The Country I Remember*, was published in 1996 and won the Poetry Society of America's Alice Fay di Castagnola Award. It is the most American of his books to date—even more so than *Ludlow*, most of whose characters are immigrants and recall their lives in Europe. *The Country I Remember* is entirely set in America, and principally in the West. Two-thirds of the book is taken up with the narrative that gives the book its title, which is based on family memoirs of combat, travel, and home-seeking during and after the Civil War. The last third contains twelve poems, one of which is another blank-verse narrative.

Frisardi has indicated the importance of "**The Country I Remember**" for Mason: "It seems that writing this long poem was concurrent with Mason's discovery of his roots and the consummation of his apprenticeship as a poet." The poet explains in *News from the Village* how he came across the material that lay behind the poem; in the 1980s, while working in Los Angeles on the unsuccessful film adaptation of his Alaskan novel, he stayed with his great-aunt, Mary Hertz, a former vaudeville dancer. "It was Mary who told me that her grandfather had fought in the Civil War and gave me stories I would later incorporate into a long, fictional poem, *The Country I Remember*" (*News*, 92). She showed Mason letters of John Mitchell and gave him a transcription of his account of being captured at Chicamagua and imprisoned at Libby. Subsequently, he stumbled across an account by John Mitchell's daughter, Maggie, of the family's journey across the country in 1880. This led him to develop the character of Maggie Gresham, who is essentially fictional; if anything, she is based more on his great-aunt, Mary Hertz, than on Mitchell's daughter.

The story therefore has two narrators, writing from different points in time. Mitchell describes his wartime experiences, including capture and escape from prison, and subsequently his striking out westward with his wife and five children for Washington Territory, where he settles on a farm, moving in old age to a town. Maggie Gresham describes how she breaks free from the family and sets off even farther west, to Portland, Oregon, and then south to California, where she meets her blacksmith husband. As Gwynn puts it, the poem "may be the truest kind of history—the recollections of those who have taken part in history without having taken part in making it" (137).

The title of the narrative, which comes from a poem

by Trumbull Stickney (both narrators are readers of the popular poets of their day), introduces us to the theme of memory—and, of course, to that of "country." It is a poem built on memories, the memories of two characters who have spent much of their lives travelling the country, with apparent restlessness, but perhaps in search of a final resting place. In this respect it is interesting to notice the opening and closing lines of the poem. The first voice we hear is that of Maggie Gresham, recalling the family's train journey across the continent:

> The rattle and sway of the train as it clattered across
> leagues of open grassland put me to sleep ...

Her father's voice closes the poem, indicating the grave where his wife already lies: "And I will rest there when my time has come." The poem thus begins with a mainly anapestic line, whose rhythm mimics the onward movement of the train, and it closes with a line of steady iambic monosyllables, effecting full closure. The last line indeed stands alone, like the last line of every section in the poem, supernumerary to the compressed seven-line stanzas in which the narrative is organized.

Given the circuitous nature of the narrative (more on this later), it is by no means perverse to begin our analysis with the final stanza, leading up to that closing line. Lieutenant Mitchell is speaking:

> I'm getting used to living here in town.
> This is my home. This is my home because

I say it is. I told you about my life
so you would know how this place is my home.
I knew I'd come back like a boy in love
and build my wife that frame house, room by room.
I knew that one of us would choose a grave.

This is typical of Mitchell's narrative style: steady and declarative, making his point by simple, forceful statements. The story may have been told in rather zig-zag fashion, but he wishes to make it clear that there has always been a well-determined goal. He builds the stanza with short, assertive sentences that consist almost exclusively of monosyllabic words, just as he has built his wife a "frame house, room by room." He has always known that this was his aim, just as he has always known that the end of all would be the grave. It is the voice of a man who knows how to adapt himself to circumstances and who can then convince himself that such circumstances were in some way intended. But perhaps most importantly, the stanza declares the importance of speech and of telling stories. It is in the telling that the pattern of things reveals itself.

Earlier he declared, "I've told these stories before, but wanted someone / to set them properly on paper, now, / in case my mind in old age starts to drift." The fear of aimless drifting is one that runs through the whole volume, as we will see; Mitchell here shows an awareness that travel is not a good in itself and can appear mere shiftlessness. He says of his own journeys, "in my day I've traveled / back and forth like a saw blade cutting wood ..." The structure of the narrative as a whole adds to this sense of back-and-forth movement, with the journeys of the father and daughter seemingly crisscrossing in continuation. We begin with the train traveling west, in classic pioneering fashion, and the "wandering tribes of old" are evoked. Maggie Gresham then tells us that it is also a return for her father: "because he'd known some part of it in youth / and memory had made him bring us back." Subsequently, when the daughter leaves the family to travel farther west, to Portland, we learn that her father had been there before her; he too had experienced its famously wet climate: "Never was a land so full of rain— / the ground soaked it up and squished when you walked." This echo of the past gives extra point to the line the daughter quotes from the Stickney poem: "it rains across the country I remember." The memory is also a familial one.

As already stated, it is a very American story. Despite the to-and-fro motion of their journeys, the overall tendency is forever westward; Maggie Gresham says at one point, "I have never grown used to trains going east." In the final section, titled "Eighty Acres," Lt. Mitchell comments on the restless pioneering spirit: "This country's always on the move. Sometimes / if you don't want to carry a great weight / you drop it and walk away. America / is made by those who want to change themselves." His daughter says in similar fashion: "As long as I was moving there was hope / that I would find the place we all had sought." Later, after a single line devoted to the death of her baby ("Our baby didn't live beyond four months"), she and her husband embark on another move:

> and Howard saw the move would do us good
> and I said, "Yes, my people always move
> when staying in one place is killing them."

But there is also a full awareness of the losses that such restlessness brings with it. After the father has recounted the move west, he adds a single sentence (again, one of those striking isolated lines): "That was the last my wife saw of her folks." Similarly, Maggie, after her move west, never sees her mother again.

Each section has its own title, and perhaps the most significant of these is the single word "Sojourners," for Lt. Mitchell's fourth section. The word comes from a sermon preached after the death of Mitchell's companion, in his early western adventures, in the 1850s:

> We had a preacher with us who could sermon:
> "For we are strangers before thee," he said,
> "and sojourners, as were all our fathers:
> our days on the earth are as a shadow and
> there is none abiding."

The image returns to his mind after he has been captured by the Confederates: "I thought of sojourners in the train's darkness, / hauled with other Union men to Richmond." It is this sense of impermanence that makes the gift of memory so important, and the act of telling one's story is one way of ensuring that something shall abide. Mitchell is unable to draw large-scale pictures of the war, but he can bear testimony to the experiences of the single soldier, caught up in events that are almost incomprehensible. As Gwynn puts it, "The most striking parts of the poem are Lt. Mitchell's recollections of the battle which describe foraging and small-unit actions in which, as in *The Red Badge of Courage*, any larger sense of the fighting is lost on men trying to find enough food and water and cover to survive" (136). Not everything can be told ("I talk a lot, but some things I can't say"), however, and one of the characteristics of Lt. Mitchell's narration is a laconic reticence or deliberate understatement with regard to his grimmest experiences:

> Some they kept
> Below in cages where they fed on rats.
> The whole business was a bit discouraging

Elsewhere he says simply, "I don't mind telling you conditions there were bad."

His daughter is highly conscious of the importance of the act of narration. It is no accident that she is the one chosen by her father to read poetry out loud: "I understood / always that I was here to be a voice." At her mother's funeral, she hears "the rustle of children" in the wooden pews and their shoes "tapping / and scraping the Lord's floorboards" and she thinks, "This is life going on, this is the form / of memory, the way our voices will remain." The phrase "form of memory" is rather mysterious but seems to be associated with the sounds of the children; perhaps more significantly, it is again associated with the word "voices."

The most memorable form of speech is, of course, poetry. Father and daughter, as already stated, share a love of the popular poets of the day. Stickney provides the title and is cited several times. Longfellow, however, is clearly the favorite of both father and daughter; indeed, it even seems that the daughter accepts Howard Gresham's proposal of marriage because she recalls the lines from Longfellow's poem describing the blacksmith: "Those were lines my Papa used to love." Poetry can evoke sunshine amid the rain of Portland: "I learned that I must first talk to myself / retelling stories, muttering a few / remembered lines of verse, to make the earth / substantial and to bring the sunlight back." Elsewhere we are told that Maggie reads Whitman to her father (something that may strike us as a little less likely). And her father shows an awareness of the great classics, evoking Homer: "no, nothing like that old Greek, / Achilles, who we read about at school." Verse is not always a panacea, however. It is powerless when her baby dies: "I tried to summon up my old belief / or find some verse that would relieve the pain, / but life won't always come when it is called." Poetry is here directly associated with life (as in the title of Mason's first book of essays).

Despite the frequent reference to voices, there is in fact an underlying sense of the impossibility of communicating. The two speakers are not talking to each other. Mason has said, "Part of the tragic element in my poem, it seems to me, is the isolation of these two voices, almost as if they were speaking into a vast silence." The title of the fourth section, "Acoustic Shadows," seems to have a relevance beyond the specific circumstances of the battle where the phenomenon is described. Mrs. Gresham, who is the more reflective of the two, after describing the loneliness of "listening to that driving rain," says:

> Maybe that is why we go on talking,
> always trying to show someone we're here,
> and look—I have a past just like you do,
> a stream of words that fills the empty night
> and sweetens troubled dreams, or so we hope.

Her voice is as unstoppable but perhaps also as meaningless as the rain. She is aware too of those whose voices never get heard: "No one ever wrote down Mama's stories." And in her final section (which takes its title from Longfellow, "The Children's Hour"), she ruefully declares her sense of frustration: "to have so much to say and no one here / to say it to." The niece who calls to take her out for drives is more interested in talking about her own problems, and ironically it is to the sound of her prattling voice that Mrs. Gresham's final reflections take shape:

> and while I listened, all at once I heard
> the hoofbeats of the surf come pounding in.
> I thought it was the voice of memory

> crashing and flowing down across the earth,
> and underneath, like roots that probe for water,
>
> and I was moved by everything that moved.

This image connects with an earlier evocation of water:

> I thought my whole ambition was to make
> the past and present come together, dreamed
> into a vivid shape that memory
> could hold the way the land possesses rivers.
> They in turn possess the land and carry it
> in one clear stream of thought to drink from
> or water gardens with.

The image is undeniably suggestive but at first sight may seem a little confused: one finds oneself asking whether memory is the water or the land. But then one realizes that it is, in fact, the apparent confusion that is so richly evocative, as it hints at the way past and present do live together in our minds—which is to say, the way memory works.

Frisardi says in his essay, "Mason tells his story in a naturalistic manner (there are remarkably few metaphors or similes in his narrative poems)—with the blend of American speech rhythms and blank verse that he has mastered." This is generally true of the narrative poems. But in the case of "The Country I Remember," we notice the way certain natural images take on symbolic resonance. Throughout the poem, water is a recurring image: the rain of Portland, the rivers of the continent, the thirst of the soldiers, and the ocean in Mrs. Gresham's final reflections. The poem ranges widely over the continent, but the key feature that distinguishes the different landscapes is always the presence or absence of water. In an essay on Heaney and Frost, Mason writes (echoing Elizabeth Bishop), "Our experience may often be fragmentary, yet we may also believe that reality is not fragmented, a wholeness just beyond our ken. One apparently universal image of this principle is water, flowing and flown, changing and stable, clear and sustaining" (*Poetry of Life*, 94). It is through such subtle imagery that the poem, despite presenting two voices separated by time and by geography, despite the constant shifts in time and space, achieves a kind of subliminal unity. It is our sense that both Mrs. Gresham and Lt. Mitchell, for all their apparent drifting, are in search of this "wholeness beyond our ken" that makes their stories so touching. "River Days," a poem in his later volume, *Sea Salt*, concludes with a stanza that could serve as a coda to the two interwoven stories.

> Like others of our kind we move toward water,
> not only to slake our thirst
> but also because it binds us,
> our tides and metamorphoses, our bed
> of scars, our love, our passing.

The last third of the book contains twelve poems, only one of which extends beyond two pages (another narrative, "The Escape"). The poems are greatly varied in form and in theme, but there are certain recurring elements. The title of one of the poems provides a clue to the prevailing mood: **"Three Characters from a Lost Home."** We have a general impression that the characters in these poems are abandoned or adrift in a world they struggle to make sense of.

The three characters from a lost home are Cedar, Water, and Woodsmoke. Each of them acts as speaker in a tetrameter sonnet. The first speaker, Cedar, may make an immediate impression of solidity and rootedness, but the sonnet lays greater emphasis on the tree's "secrets" and its mysterious "green intelligence." It concludes with the line "I grow unmoving till I die," suggesting that there is something fatal in excessive immobility. The sonnets of Water and Woodsmoke present more characteristic images of things drifting and unraveling. In the concluding lines of the trio of poems, Woodsmoke announces its departure from its "burning home": "I drift out of stone / into the woods alone." In the final line of the second sonnet, Water declares that it will "rejoin / the gallery of clouds above a lake" and "wait for my unravelling." The line seems to echo the final line of the first poem in this section, **"El Rio de las Animas Perdidas en Purgatorio,"** in which the poet writes about his ancestors, saying that his people's time beside the River Purgatoire "was brief—far briefer than our scattering." Later we will hear about the poet's own marriage unraveling, while in one of the elegies that conclude the book, we read that the ashes of his brother are allowed to "drift over the heather."

The first poem, already cited in the opening chapter,

moves from a meditation on the Spanish explorers, whose "armored bones" gave rise to the river's striking name, to the poet's ancestors, who "came here when the coal mines started" and "fed their young on Rockefeller's scrip," an allusion that will become clear to readers of *Ludlow*. The poem opens with a line describing the failure of memory: "No one recollects where the Spaniards died." The reference to their "armored bones" is a powerful image of the futility of human precautions. Mason is making it his business to recollect the Spaniards, to give them the more enduring armor of poetry, and subsequently to bring together the scattered remains of family memories. He admits that he has "never been to see their graves" (something he will remedy when he comes to write *Ludlow*), but the lines of his poem serve as some kind of memorial.

As these two poems suggest, the section contains a characteristic mixture of fictional narratives and personal recollections, loosely connected by an overall sense of loss and of things "unravelling." The landscapes are American and predominantly wintry or bleak. The poem "**In the Northern Woods**," for example, describes the discovery of the corpse of an unidentified girl by a lake. It is not only the landscape that recalls the poetry of Robert Frost, but also the emphasis given to the harsh uncaringness of nature. The changes wrought by the seasons ("winter drifts against a cabin door / and change comes quickly on a southern breeze") are huge, impersonal forces that make human lives seem irrelevant. The final lines—"the birds will tell us nothing of her worth / whose small bones left no imprint on the earth"—suggest that the girl's bones are as tiny and ephemeral as those of the birds themselves. As H. L. Hix put it, "the tragedy lies not in the poet's own grief, but in the fact that the girl's story will never be told, that she will remain as 'anonymous as leaves along the shore'" (210). The tender rhyming couplet that closes the poem appears to be an attempt to memorialize her, even in her anonymity.

In "**Old House**," a poem with rhyming stanzas of mingled pentameter and dimeter, another anonymous figure, this time an old woman, is observed by children as the ghostlike inhabitant of a house that seems as frail and precarious as its owner. The curiously shaped stanzas themselves seem to hint at the tottering state of both the building and its inhabitant. As in Frost's "Directive," the woods encroach menacingly upon the home; after the woman's death, the house simply "vanished in cascading weeds and vines," a grim lesson in mortality to the children.

An even more desperately lost figure is the protagonist of "**The Escape**," which Mason has declared was inspired by a short newspaper item. It is Mason's first narrative poem in the third person. The protagonist, who appears to have escaped from a mental hospital, has something in common with the figure of Benjy in *The Sound and the Fury*. Like Benjy, he confuses times and places: "Faces come and go in the moving rooms / but he can't remember any of their names." In particular, he has no sense of causal relations: "Nobody tells him why this has to happen. / *What did I do to you?* he wants to know." It is up to the reader to try to stitch together his confused and fragmented memories of home and the home. The confusion is also one of perspective; we, like the protagonist, are never sure of whether things are close or far, either in space or time, and we have to work out his actions from the shifts in angle of vision. "All the sudden he's taller than the fence," we are told at one point. And then, "The fence stares down on him from a long ways ..." And later, "Now the fence is gone ..." In this indirect and jerky fashion, we attempt to follow his movements.

The protagonist is clearly referred to as a man, but his thought processes are childlike, and many of the memories seem to be of himself as a child, although they are confusingly reported in the present tense. One abiding memory seems to be that of a "switch," which he recalls "trying to balance [...] in his open palm," and which was carried off by a hound and then used against him: "He feels the switch come down across his back." The poem ends with him lying down helplessly in the cold black soil, suddenly aware that "the hound is long, long dead" and waiting "for the whipping that will surely come." The sudden acquisition of temporal awareness, of things having happened irrevocably in the past, brings with it a sense of utter hopelessness for the future.

Childhood is a recurring theme in the book. It has little to do with Wordsworthian notions of splendor in the grass or glory in the flower. "**The Summer of Love**," written in jaunty ballad stanzas, recalls a holiday camp in the 1960s and beautifully re-creates the sense of liberation felt by the children; the setting is evoked with well-chosen period details ("we liked the underwater voice / of 'Yellow Submarine'"). At the heart of the story, however, is the tragedy of a scoutmaster who goes mad. The subsequent three days spent by the children with no adult supervision are closer to *Lord of the Flies* than *Coral Island*: "With no adult, what savages / we were!" One is reminded of the tormented crabs of an earlier holiday poem, "In the Islands." At the same time, we are made aware of a whole world of adult madness that lies beyond their island: "The world of grown-ups seemed awash / in trouble; some took pills, // some gassed themselves in their garages." And a parenthesis offers historical perspective, by pointing out that the "Summer of Love / was the summer of the damned; / sixteen thousand American boys / had died in Viet Nam." The defiantly upbeat ending of the poem, in a stanza extended to six lines, thus seems distinctly ironic, with its reference to "the feeling that summer never ends / and we would never lose."

The unrhyming sonnet that immediately follows, "**Land without Grief**," is another evocation of childhood, but this time a more intimate, family-based one. Mason pictures an agnostic childhood, with a family who on "Sundays went skiing on the mountain / while others knelt in church." The description of the defiantly outdoor and nondevotional activities "beneath cold blizzard vaults of heaven" recalls the penultimate stanza of Wallace Stevens's "Sunday Morning," where traditional religious worship is replaced with "boisterous devotion to the sun," with the full support of the "trees like serafin, and echoing hills, / That choir among themselves long afterward." Just as Stevens's poem ends with the ambiguous image of pigeons descending "to darkness on extended wings," so Mason's sonnet, after offering an apparent vision of security, with the child dozing "in the damp wool smell / and murmur of grown-up talk inside the car," concludes with a decidedly less reassuring image of "oncoming dark / probed by descending cars with lighted beams."

The most famous poem in the book, "**Song of the Powers**," has been widely anthologized. It was apparently written with children in mind; Mason has said that the poem came to him when he "was teaching an Adrienne Rich poem called 'Power' and a student mentioned that it reminded her of that children's game" ("Mundane Question," Eratosphere). He was "struck by the observation, and almost immediately after class began to meditate on that game, hearing a strong, two-beat rhythm in [his] head." With its refrain-like repetitions and insistent pulsing beat, one could think of it as a particularly grim nursery rhyme; this, together with its universally familiar subject matter, has undoubtedly contributed to its success.

The emphatic beat of the verse makes each voice—that of stone, of paper, and of scissors—sound egotistically in-

sistent, right from the repeated word "Mine," which opens
the first two lines of the first three stanzas. In the final
stanza, the stress instead falls on the words *all* and *alone*,
in the repeated line "all end alone." And so, after three
stanzas of solipsistic myopia, the last stanza ends with an
external, imperative voice, urging universal destruction:

> So heap up your paper
> and scissor your wishes
> and uproot the stone
> from the top of the hill.
> They all end alone
> as you will, you will.

The final lines turn outward, presumably to address the
reader menacingly. Mason has said that the poem "has a
vitality and freshness and memorability worth keeping"
but confesses himself "a bit appalled by the darkness of its
message" ("Mundane Question," Eratosphere).

   "The Pond" describes a return to a place last visited
with a lover twenty years earlier. Frisardi has said that the
poem reenacts "the fluid interplay between perception of
the present and the ghosts of the past." But the contrast
between the remembered summer and the present winter
("Tonight the temperature is due to fall, / an arctic stillness settle on the prairies ...") adds an extra touch of unreality to the evocation of the past; as Frisardi puts it, there
is the awareness that memory's prolongation of time and
experience is itself ephemeral and vaporous: "The years
slow down and look about for shelter / far from forests

and far from summer ponds: / the mind ghosting out in a shoal of stars."

The next poem, "**This Is Your Gift**," is devoted to the experience of sleeping beside a lover. The poem consists principally of questions that seem to find no answers, exploring the mystery of the paradoxical combination of intimacy and separateness that is part of the experience. River imagery runs through the poem, which uses an agile anapestic rhythm to convey a sense of fluid movement. The ambiguity of the poem can be seen even in its title, which leaves it unclear whether the "you" that is being addressed is the donor or receiver of the gift. The question is raised in the penultimate line: "What has been given? What has been lost?" The final line hints at a response: "Breathe with the body beside you and know."

The last two poems in the book return to the theme of his brother's death. "**Letter to No Address**," in rhyming quatrains, addresses his dead brother directly, recalling the carefree days of their early childhood. He beautifully evokes their boyish energy amid a wild landscape: "Brother, I want to map the old hardscrabble / places we ransacked, bluffs or high above." The imagery of mountain exploration continues into the next stanza, but the last line of the stanza suddenly introduces an alien concept: "but storms could not prepare us for divorce." In the next stanza, the outdoor imagery becomes abruptly and starkly figurative: "The route, chosen without our consent, / abandoned children in a wilderness ..." It might seem even too obvious a metaphor, but its blunt unambiguousness has its own rude force: it jerks us into an awareness of the sense of total bewilderment felt by the children in these new circumstances. The last three stanzas deal with the breakup of the family as the brothers go their separate ways; Mason tells us that his own "love unraveled / far from the woods and mountains that we knew."

We return to the fatal climb in the penultimate stanza; the first three lines address Doug, and the final line describes Mason's reaction to the tragedy in a short, declarative sentence: "When I recall that instant I go numb." The final stanza is an expression of utter helplessness in the face of grief, an admission of the inefficacy of poetry in the face of such tragedy: "I live in a world too full of elegies, / and find no compensation in these lines …" It is clear that Mason is not playing some postmodern game here, slyly undercutting the authority of the poem. These lines simply and devastatingly express his feelings.

The last poem in the book, "**A Motion We Cannot See**," describes the return of the poet with his surviving brother and his father to the spot in the mountains where they had scattered Doug's ashes a year earlier. It is an event that Mason has described in his prose memoir, with slightly different emphasis, concluding with his father's words.

"This isn't him," my father finally said. "I don't know where he is, but this isn't Doug." And he waved a hand at the air, signifying where Doug had gone.[1]

1. In a later poem, "Energy" (included in *Sea Salt*), Mason recalls a friend of

The poem provides a fitting end to this book, so centered on questions of home and homelessness, roving and rootedness. The three men return to the place where they "had cupped / the ashes, letting them blow / and drift over the heather." It had seemed all too appropriate a destiny for a mountain lover. Mason asks, "what could be left of him, / so utterly possessed by mountains?" The phrase is heartbreaking.

The final stanza persists with the notion of possession: "The prayers / of blizzard and snowmelt have him now . . ." After all the various images of drifting and transience that have characterized the volume, the book ends with the mysterious but perhaps distantly reassuring image of time that "flows down the mountain like the ice." This is the "motion we cannot see" that gives the poem its title. The very last line maintains the quality of mystery: "though it bears our blood almost forever." The "almost" is the surprising element here; it seems to indicate a determination to resist to the last the religious comfort implicit in the notion of eternity.

---

his father, Dewey Huston, who "had an explanation where he'd gone, / waving a hand in air. *It's energy, /* you said. *That energy must still be somewhere.*"

CHAPTER 5

Arrivals

Coming after *The Country I Remember*, Mason's new volume immediately strikes the reader by its international scope. The poems take us all over the planet, reaching even as far as New Zealand. A closer reading also reveals how marine imagery washes through the book, with descriptions and evocations of the open sea and of shorelines, of stormy seas and calm ones, of the Mediterranean and the Pacific. Even the land itself is described at times as if it were the sea (in the case of New Zealand, as indicated in the verse letter from that country, this makes etymological sense). Conversely, there seems to be a persistent search for anchorings and safe landings (the book's title is significant), for solidity and rootedness, as with the image of the cedar tree in "A Meaning Made of Trees": "the hulking host, / and omphalos of my dream world."

Along with the search for safe arrivals, we notice a growing interest in the theme of identity: both the possibly liberating experience of shedding it ("why can't you lose yourself on Nehru Road?"), the mysteries of its fragmentation ("Small Steps"), and the desire to define it and fix it—or at least the desire to understand whether such fixity is possible (or indeed desirable). A number of poems play with the theme of nomenclature ("A Mountain Saxifrage" and "A Birthday") as a way of fixing things, and in general, there is an awareness of the slipperiness of language—which also means an awareness of the need to take full advantage of its protean possibilities in writing of a changeable world.

The theme of "loss" is a recurring one, with the figure of Edward Lear in the first section perhaps best expressing the paradoxical truth at the heart of the book: "He is the sum of all that he has lost, / his hand still dreaming on the empty page." These lines, the final ones in this touching portrait of the Victorian artist and poet, are emblematic in their twofold significance. On the one hand, they testify movingly to the sad loneliness of this eccentric figure; on the other, they testify to a sense of the eternal possibility of new beginnings. What is important is to use those empty pages to record the dreams—including the failed dreams and the losses. Even such tragic losses as those of a father's memory deserve to be recorded: "the inarticulate / we try to voice before it is too late" ("New Zealand Letter").

Section 1: The Dream of Arrival

In the opening poem of the book, a translation of Cavafy's **"The City,"** Mason makes an interesting decision in the very first line, translating the word *thalassa* as "shore" rather than "sea." This anomalous choice, which does not seem to be driven solely by rhyme, finds a curious echo in the title of the penultimate poem in the book, "Swimmers on the Shore" (which is also the name of the entire last section).

Frisardi noticed Mason's decision to open the book with the translation of this poem, which "is about the uselessness and futility of the geographical cure for chronic dissatisfaction": "Now that you have decided you are through / with this place, you've wrecked your life everywhere." This serves as a response to Maggie Gresham's remark, "Yes, my people always move / when staying in one place is killing them." A warning note is thus struck at the beginning of a book that is characterized by the restless travel of "chronic dissatisfaction."

Cavafy also serves as a natural introduction to the sequence of Greek poems that follow. Interesting light can be thrown on some of these poems by comparing them with passages from the prose memoir of his time in Greece; some of the poems are included in the book itself. Reading *News from the Village*, we can see that the poems come from different periods of Mason's life. "On the Terrace" is clearly connected with an event during his first stay in Greece; "Kalamitsi" describes his return to the village after sixteen years; "Gulls in the Wake" derives from one of his frequent trips to Greece with students.

The sequence begins with "**In Transit**," a rather mysterious poem that broods on the urge to drift. The opening sentence seems to imitate the roaming spirit, wandering over five lines, with a series of loosely connected images of inconclusive purposelessness ("when days have no more purpose than a song / at midnight [...] or books you packed but cannot seem to read"). The wandering figure seems to be contrasted with "those who aimed for work," who have "dull eyes." Just a few lines later, however, we learn that the traveler, too, has "jaded sight." Islands (a recurring image in Mason's poetry) seem to be symbols of allurement. "Islands, more islands than you could name, / lay like lovers at morning: *Don't leave. Stay.*" But in the next lines, the islands seem to be connected with the myth of Atlantis, suggesting the impossibility of ever finding satisfaction.

The last stanza evokes the figure of the Gorgóna, a figure from Greek folktales; in an essay on Seferis, Mason tells us that the poet decorated the title page of his collection with a drawing of this figure:

In Greek folklore the sister of Alexander the Great had been transformed into this vengeful creature. If a fisherman caught her in his net, she would challenge him with a question: "Where is Alexander the Great?" The poor fisherman had to answer properly—"Alexander the Great lives and reigns"—or the Gorgóna would swamp his boat and send him to Davy Jones. (*Two Minds*, 155)

As he remarks in *News from the Village*, after observing that Patrick Leigh Fermor has a tattoo of this figure, "It was the ultimate parable of modern Greek identity" (298). In this poem, however, the figure is evoked as "a fisherman's fantasy," who leaves the observer in a "turmoil of desire." The concluding line of the poem is wryly ambiguous: "You are as happy as you'll ever be."

The next poem, "**Gulls in the Wake**," is the closest Mason comes to writing a religious poem. The episode is also described in *News from the Village*, where we learn that Mason was accompanying a group of students from Kos to Piraeus on Easter night. The prose description is close to the poem for the most part, relating how he responded to the joyful announcement of two passengers—"Christ is risen!"—observed rockets "from the coast near Sounion," heard the singing of cantors and priests broadcast by radio from a church in Athens, and finally observed the gulls in the wake of the ship. The greatest variation is in the tone of the description of this last event. In the prose version, Mason describes the gulls as "ghostly presences" and then asks, "Were they flesh or spirit? Was this an annunciation or merely a crowd of refugees seeking a free meal?" He then adds, almost by way of ironic afterthought, "The whole encounter damned near made a Christian out of me."

The tone in the poem is different. The final stanza reads:

> And that was when I saw them—ghostly, winged,
> doggedly following outside our light,
> hopeful without a thought of hope, feeding
> and diving to feed in waves I could not see.

The gulls are not named as such, since they have been a presence in the poem from the title. Even so, the choice of using only a pronoun allows the notion of the ineffable to enter the poem. They are framed within two contrasting clauses, "I saw them" and "I could not see," which add to the sense of mystery. The words "Hopeful without a thought of hope" perhaps recall St. Paul's description of Abraham, thus turning the gulls into an image of religious faith, able to take sustenance from unseen sources. Mason does not force us into an allegorical reading of the image; he closes the poem with it, leaving us to ponder how shaky the foundations of most beliefs are, including agnosticism.

As if determined to break the spell of mystery, Mason follows this quasi-mystical meditation with a twelve-line poem, "**Schoolchildren at Mistras**," celebrating the vitality of careless youth. Set in the ancient but abandoned Byzantine town of Mistras, the poem for ten lines evokes a sense of age and reverent silence ("A hush ascends the ruined holy city . . ."), only to break it with the joyous irruption of children's voices: "silence these schoolchildren happily shatter, / as if escaping death in the museum."

"**On the Terrace**" is a far more personal work and returns to an episode from his early stay in Greece, with his first wife. The episode—simply the observation with friends of the sudden and surprising mating of two owls—is one that is recalled in his prose memoir. In the prose account, the episode comes at the end of a chapter describing the couple's friendship with two other foreigners in the village. The event occurs suddenly during a "lingering evening in spring," and the four of them, once the birds have flown away, look "at each other with a wild surmise." The Keatsian allusion suggests a moment of sudden revelation, but the next moment, things are resolved in laughter. Mason hints at the tensions within the couples only in indirect fashion in the chapter's final paragraph, describing the sun setting over the village, which then "settled down to its uneasy truce, a whole history of feuds and alliances hidden behind its gray stone walls."

The poem, written in tightly rhyming trimeter quatrains, creates the same "lingering" mood for the first five stanzas, assisted by the "resinous wine" of the opening line. The owls burst in on the poem in noisy and openly comic fashion, rather like the children in the holy city of the previous poem: "Her mate lands at her tail / and old tile rooftops clatter. / She puts up such a wail / we wonder what's the matter." The feminine rhymes add to the effect of raucous comedy. But the final three stanzas of the poem shift register and tone markedly. Here, the look is exchanged only between the speaker and his lover: "a look I can't erase // because I'll never know / if it was love or hate." In the last stanza, Mason adopts one of his characteristic shifts of temporal perspective (see "In the Islands," for example); with its short, end-stopped lines and simple rhymes, the stanza suddenly sounds like an epitaph for his failed marriage.

Our laughter dies with the light.
The owls and friends depart.
Decades have taken flight,
and we were wrong from the start.

The poem that follows, **"Kalamitsi,"** describes a key moment in Mason's life: his return to the little house by the bay after sixteen years. The poem is included in the prose memoir; indeed, one almost feels it makes the previous page of prose description redundant. In the context of the poetry volume, the poem at once gives meaning to the title of the book. Kalamitsi becomes the symbol of all those longed-for arrivals that are so important in a life of constant travel. In this case, of course, it is also a return, and a reassuring one, suggesting that some things do remain constant. The poem proceeds by simple statements of fact, which pinpoint time and location with careful precision: "The path I had not walked for sixteen years ..."; "two steps down where it rounded the bay / and I was back."

The poem celebrates "the small survivals" of certain elemental things: the stone wall, the gate, the little house, the cool spring. Mason confers a sense of essentiality on these things, recalling the "spring that is the water of the house" in Frost's "Directive." In the opening line of the last stanza, we realize that it is his own survival that is at issue as well: "I had come through to see this much again ..." The phrase "this much" might seem ironic; indeed, he emphasizes the outward insignificance of the "small survivals" yet further by devoting the last stanza entirely to the most rudimentary and basic object of all: a plank bench placed under a cypress tree "all those years ago / to soak up shade on summer afternoons." The poem ends with a line that is a triumph of quiet understatement: "only a small plank bench, but quite enough." The passage from the almost ironic "this much" to the solaced "quite enough" is touching.

The poem is related to another short Greek narrative, "*Agnostos Topos*," which is placed toward the end of the first section, after a cluster of international poems. "*Agnostos Topos*" evokes the first sight of the village, even though the tense of the first verb ("We had walked ...") indicates at once that this moment of first sight is being recalled from a later standpoint. Much of the effect of the poem comes from the contrast between the primitive isolation of the village on that first visit and its present-day connectedness. The viewpoint is frankly nostalgic. He re-creates the exact feelings of that first arrival, including the thirst and heat of the travelers. By recalling the rough approach, beautifully evoked in lines thick with consonantal clusters—"salt-stung, dusty, like summer's rasping grass / and the roughness of stone"—he emphasizes the absence of a road. This primitive condition is made picturesquely clear in the response to the travelers' question about the distance to the nearest road: "*Two cigarettes,* / said the old man who sat webbing his net."

The next line, as plain and direct as the road it refers to, shatters this impression of quaint seclusion: "Now the road cuts down from the cliffs above." While acknowledging that this connection has its obvious benefits ("One needn't stare a lifetime at hot cliffs, / thinking them impassable except to goats"), the poet clearly mourns what has been lost. The mourning becomes a general regret for the passing years in the final stanza; indeed, they become the *agnostos topos*, or unknown country, of the title. The poem ends with a recollection of that sense of arrival he once felt—a recollection that is all the more moving from the implied contrast with the displaced present:

> Yet how like home it seemed when I walked down
> out of the unfenced hills, thirsty, footsore,
> with words of greeting for the fisherman.

The other travel poems in the first section are more openly touristic. The three Indian poems convey the frank bemusement of the western visitor amid an exotic but disconcerting culture. "**Mumbai**" uses the form of the ghazal, with its insistent repetends, to communicate the sense of overwhelming sensory stimulation; the repeated place name ("Nehru Road") that terminates each couplet comes to seem like a desperate attempt on the part of the poet to maintain his bearings in a bewildering world. The final couplet ironically castigates his stubborn hanging onto his western identity: "Mason, you've come to the other side of the world— / why can't you lose yourself on Nehru Road?"

In the sonnet "**A Beggar of Chennai**," Mason, observing a crippled beggar, muses on the arbitrariness of life, as it doles out fortune or misfortune. The image of the arm-less beggar flipping "the coin from the bone knob / into his mouth" acts as a cruelly apt metaphor of the concept that life is ruled by "a gambling god." The final four lines describe the traffic that hides the boy from sight, suggesting ironically that there is some design to it—and Mason underscores the notion by introducing the only rhyme in the entire poem: "headlong, woven by invisible hands / so multiple I could not count the strands."

The last Indian poem, "**Towers of Silence**," constitutes a frank admission of the superficiality of the tourist view of the country, providing a frantic series of almost meaningless glimpses of various aspects of Indian life. We are told in a single line, "Everything's recycled. Every life is short." The poem endeavors to reproduce this impression of untiring cyclical movement and provisionality, passing from one image to another, like the birds that feed on the corpses on the "Towers of Silence," which then "appear in photographs / of unsuspecting tourists like yourself, / or sail with equanimity above / commuter trains, apartment blocks, hotels." The enduring message of the poem would seem to be the brusque opening line of the last stanza, "You are not here for long," which appears to be addressed laconically to the superficial tourist and rather more fatalistically to the inhabitants of the subcontinent.

We return to Europe with the next two poems, one set in Scotland and the other in Ireland. "**The Chambered Cairn**," dedicated to Annie Lennox, offers a portrait of two aged relatives of the poet's wife, of widely differing temperaments. The poem ends with a meditation on Annie's position, "Thinking Ayrshire, speaking American, / you cannot even say where you belong." The last stanza recalls both the buried houses of his first volume of poems, as it compares her broken family to "a chambered cairn / you found on Arran," and the "scattering" of the poet's own family, as evoked in "El Rio de las Animas Perdidas in Purgatorio," with just "a few skewed bones to mark the burials."

"**Limerick Junction**" describes a train journey in Ireland during which the carousing of "raucous boys" reminds the poet of his own "youth in the sixties." Perhaps in subliminal homage to the comic verse form evoked by the title, he uses a jaunty trimeter stanza (with more abundant use of trisyllabic feet than the similar stanza form of "On the Terrace") to express a sense of displacement, which clearly has its enjoyable side. He asks himself the eternal rueful question, "How could it seem so long ago / yet hardly long enough?" Accepting the compulsory respectability that comes with middle age, when the future is "at my back," he confines himself to breathing "the last illegal smoke" of the boys' joints "and settle[s] for hot tea."

"**New Zealand Letter**" is a charmingly rambling verse letter with irregular rhymes addressed to his friends Anne Stevenson and Peter Lucas. The themes of restlessness and change recur, but as with the Irish poem, in light fashion, the poet, as tourist, unashamedly revels in the exotic differences of the landscape, its changefulness and its wonderful excesses:

> Begin with the region's young geology,
> the accident of islands that still rise
> and spiral into zig-zag mountain ranges,
> glaciers long and white as wizards' beards,
> cold rivers, silt green or so transparent
> they flow like breezes blowing over stones.

Everything here seems to in a state of constant transformation; what is solid becomes wisplike and magical ("wizards' beards"), and what is fluid becomes airy. The long, proliferating sentences, crammed with lists of the exotic flora and fauna, testify to the marvelous abundance of nature. He passes naturally from the flora and fauna to the "swelling towns / like Auckland, Napier, Christchurch, Wellington," which he describes as if they were just as fruitful, protean and variform as the natural phenomena of the islands.

The last stanza is the most interesting. It begins: "Yet the never-far-off sea still models change / like that wind I started with, to rearrange / Aoteroa, land of the white cloud."[1] In this disarming, self-referential manner, Mason provides a reason for the loose structure of his poem; he and the sea and the wind are in harmony, in their acceptance of change as the abiding force in the world. With

---

1. In a discussion of this poem on the website Eratosphere, Mason acknowledges that his spelling was incorrect; it should be Aotearoa.

equal equanimity, he adopts the Maori name for the land, acknowledging that nomenclature can be no more fixed than anything else. The last lines sum up this philosophy of metamorphosis beautifully, indicating the need to

> see the earth for what it is,
> not as the perfect dream that always dies,
> the Promised Land promoted in brochures,
> but as the sort of matter that endures
> by changing. Some of its forms we recognize;
> others astonish—the inarticulate
> we try to voice before it is too late,
> this metamorphic world, tidal and worn,
> rooted, adrift, alive, and dying to be born.

There is perhaps no better key to the rich paradoxes of his poetry. It certainly helps to explain his fascination with contrasting images of mobility and stasis, of restlessness and rootedness. In some ways it could be said to expand on Stevens's dictum, "Death is the mother of beauty." Like Stevens, Mason accepts that no there is no "perfect dream" that "has endured / As April's green endures." The last line, which he allows to swell into hexameter, is a rich and witty celebration of the cycles of life and death.

The section concludes with the poem that provides its title: "**The Dream of Arrival.**" Suitably, he brings the first section of the book around full circle, concluding with a poem that alludes to Cavafy's poem on journeying to Ithaca—or rather, not concluding. As Frisardi has noted, at the end of the poem, "Mason intentionally omits the closing punctuation; as in Cavafy's poem, inconclusiveness is the nature of the journey":

> Always preparing to arrive,
> I suffer the deaths of many friends,
> survive, surprised to be alive.
> My story's told, but never ends

Section 2: The Collector's Tale

The second section of the book is devoted to a verse narrative, generally agreed to be one of Mason's finest. "**The Collector's Tale**" differs from any of the first-person narratives Mason had written to that date; although he had often used voices different from his own, it was usually possible to relate them in some way to his own life: the characters were based on people he either knew well or was related to. In "The Collector's Tale," he seems to have deliberately sought people with whom he has nothing in common. To use his own description of the two speaking characters, "One is a rhyming gay shop owner, the other an itinerant halfbreed collector and drunkard who speaks in blank verse" ("Dramatic Voice," Eratosphere).

The narrative nonetheless is not out of keeping within the collection, since its central theme is that of displacement: the first speaker, the shop owner, is jolted violently from his comfortable position with "composed society" by the sudden arrival of Foley. The latter recounts the story of his having murdered Rasher, another collector, in a fit of drunken rage, after having seen the man's most precious hidden trophy: "a black man's head with eyes sewn shut" converted to an ashtray. It is a dark, disturbing story, suggesting the unconfessable violence that lies beneath the surface of American society, even where it appears most "composed" and refined.

The clash of narrative styles, indicated visually by the irruption of Foley's italicized blank verse within the smoother rhyming stanzas of the other unnamed narrator, is an indication of the seething societal and racial conflicts that the story explores. The opening stanza gives us a clear indication of the narrator's character:

> When it was over I sat down last night,
> shaken, and quite afraid I'd lost my mind.
> The objects I have loved surrounded me
> like friends in such composed society
> they almost rid the atmosphere of fright.
> I collected them, perhaps, as one inclined
> to suffer other people stoically.

The precise, qualifying diction ("quite afraid") and the neat sentences, as carefully composed as the collection of objects around himself, indicate the man's refined cast of mind and his sense of orderliness, as well as his aesthetic preference for objects over people. The opening words ("When it was over") give a false sense of closure; as will become clear, the story is far from over, and nothing is going to restore his sense of safe seclusion; the "almost" in the fifth line is crucial.

As he begins his story, our first impression is that what has disturbed him is simply Foley's presence, with "the smell of bourbon for his calling card." He offers a series of reasons for the distaste he feels for the man: "his taste as tacky as they come, / his Indian ethic perfectly absurd." His portrait of Foley, complete with witty Shakespearean allusions ("He learned to tell a real toma- / hawk from a handsaw"), is a masterpiece of fastidiously selective description, designed to bring out his own superior refinement. He says stoically, "I endured his leaning up against my oak / credenza" and notes that Foley "didn't mind the brand" of brandy he serves, nor "that I served it in a water glass." But then come the first reported words of Foley, within the final line of one of the narrator's elaborate rhyming stanzas:

I killed him, Foley said. *You got to know.*

And suddenly we are in a whole new world. Foley tells his story in blank verse, in a loose torrent of colloquial English, laced with frequent obscenities. Foley, too, has his taste in art, but he expresses his dislikes with more vigorous contempt. He lists the junk in Rasher's store, concluding with "*a blue-eyed Jesus framed / in bottlecaps—I mean he had everything / but paint-by-number sunsets.*"

The framing narrator listens to Foley's apparently rambling tale, wondering whether he should call the police. Foley's language already seems to have contaminated his own, as he thinks: "I wouldn't mind if 'fucking' Foley fried." The finical inverted commas around the alliterative obscenity are characteristic.

The description of the horrific trophy comes as a powerful shock, and Foley's rage is convincing: "*Some fucker cared just how he dried that head / and stitched the skin and cut the hole in the top— / big medicine for a man who liked cigars.*" It is hard not to feel some sympathy for Foley's reaction to this trophy to racial hatred and violence: "*I knew some things had to be destroyed.*"

The narrator himself is clearly jolted from his position of purely snobbish or aesthetic disapproval of Foley; in the penultimate stanza, he actually becomes "poor Foley." He feels as though the story has undermined everything he believes in: "Nothing of mine was inhumane, although / I felt death in a kind of undertow / pulling my life away." The tidal metaphor is interesting, suggesting a force tugging him irresistibly away from his comfortable, secluded existence toward a life of "bitter fame," as he puts it (the allusion to Sylvia Plath is curious). In the last stanza, he reports how he has done all he can to restore his home to its pristine state prior to Foley's arrival: "I've mopped the floor, washed up, moved pots of flowers / to places that he touched." But nothing can restore his equanimity. "If I believed / I would say Foley had emerged from hell. / I ask for help, but the silent house demurs." As one might expect, he muffles his desperate assessment of Foley's menace within a conditional clause. The very last word of the poem is characteristically literary; he has lost his bearings but not his pretensions.

Section 3: In the Borrowed House

The third section takes its title from the first poem, **"In the Borrowed House."** The seven poems all deal in one way or another with the theme of belonging and identity. The opening poem, epigrammatic in its tightly rhyming concision, seems to suggest that the feeling of displacement caused by staying in a "borrowed house" is enough to undermine one's very sense of identity, so that when "light's absence leans across the town, / you lay another body down." The feeling of alterity is such that even night's darkness is referred to by circumlocution.

The imagery of the sea becomes especially forceful in this section, generally connected with the notion of displacement and instability. As if to confirm by means of paradox that nothing should be taken for granted, however, the sea imagery sometimes works in unexpected fashion. For example, in the second poem in the section, about the poet's session with a therapist (the title is indeed **"The Session"**), it is the "fears" of the therapist that are described as "solid." The therapist tells the poet that if he wishes to be cured, he should renounce his poetic ambitions:

> he counters my ambition: *Let it go.*
> I almost founder on his solid fears,
> until uplifted by the undertow
> of voices whispering for three thousand years.

The image of the undertow, which swept the narrator away from his security in "The Collector's Tale," here suggests a salvific force. The 3,000 years naturally remind us of the dawn of civilization, carrying us to Mason's beloved Mediterranean, and the great tradition of classical poetry, to which he clearly feels a special tie.

In the third poem, "**Adam Speaks**," Mason adds his contribution to the well-established American tradition of Adamic poems. Roy Harvey Pearce argued that poets of the egocentric tradition, such as Whitman or Wallace Stevens, essentially celebrate their prerogative to make songs of themselves and to see and name the world; as Hoon puts it, "I was the world in which I walked, and what I saw / Or heard or felt came not but from myself" ("Tea at the Palaz of Hoon," Wallace Stevens). Mason seems to pay homage to that tradition but acknowledges that the process of self-birth is a painful one: "remember / I tore myself / out of myself, bellowing like thunder." The tone is far from triumphant. The sea imagery in this case seems to indicate an unsettling force that disturbs the ego: "There was a sea inside my flesh—I tensed / to hold it in, / but found it was the whisper of the moon / calling to me."

In "**Night Squall**," the sea imagery is clearly used as a metaphor for loss of bearings. Using the form of a dream, Mason draws on all the popular traditions of shipwreck literature, from Falconer and Coleridge to Longfellow and Poe, and perhaps even Hollywood films. He begins with the figure of "a boy manning the bridge," evoking countless images of helpless children amid the fury of the sea (Pip in *Moby Dick*, the skipper's daughter in "The Schooner Hesperus," etc.). The poem is perhaps a little too neatly allegorical, so that the images of tempestuous seas and frail barks are not quite as disturbing as might be intended. The final stanza, with its reference to the "navigator's work," reminding us of Mason's father, suggests that once again there may be family issues behind this poem. It was only later that Mason would write a poem ("Lieutenant Mason," *Sea Salt*) that deals directly with the full horrors of his father's wartime experiences.

In "**Mise en Scène**," Mason does, however, deal directly with his own experiences in Alaska. Although they cannot be compared with memories of war, they do have a notable element of violence, which is conveyed with brutal frankness. And there is an indirect but pertinent connection with the war. Mason has described his time in Alaska in prose, in the title essay of his book *The Poetry of Life*. He notes that the place he was living in, Dutch Harbor, "was a sort of garbage dump of World War II, a scavenger's paradise. I thought of it as my essential landscape—the desolate home of all literal and figurative war babies, the off-center eye of history's storm" (20).

The poem, too, has its dreamlike quality, but this time, the element of unreality comes from a sense of distorted perspective. The poem is written from the point of view of one of the crew, working "long shifts in the holds, tossing live creatures / two at a time in the lowered mesh bags."

One gets the impression that the speaker himself identifies with these doomed creatures. Above him, a crew of butchers are engaged in "killing in thousands," breaking crabs by "plung[ing] their chain-mailed chests / down on the blades." Down below, the speaker and his companions wait "for the silence between killings;" their vision of the outside world is through a "mesh," and it is only when this mesh is "full of nothing but the sky" that they can emerge to "watch the rain slant down through masts and nets." Everywhere the emphasis is on distorted or limited vision. At the end of the poem, we are told that they feel as if they themselves are being observed by the "hump-backed islands under clouds," which resemble "a pod of whales [...] spellbound to rock and heather by the scene." It is a claustrophobic poem, in which the mechanized violence takes on a hallucinatory, nightmarish tinge. Mason returned to this topic in a later poem, "Amaknak" (*Sea Salt*), which lays even greater emphasis on the violence; in the last three stanzas of this later poem, the word "Death" resounds repeatedly like a knell.

The next poem in the section, **"Ballade at 3 AM,"** makes masterly use of the ballade form to depict a number of acquaintances from the "disco Seventies." The poem reminds us that Mason missed the draft for the Vietnam war by two years. Right from the striking first line, "A Dunkin' Donuts denizen," the poem gives us a series of caustic portraits of American outcasts: dispossessed conspiracy freaks and damaged war veterans. The refrain, "I don't know where he's living now," adds to our sense of these figures as lost souls. The four lines of the envoi, with their laconic disavowal of any involvement on the poet's part ("I met them briefly, anyhow"), provide the technical resolution required by the ballade form but certainly give us no sense of satisfactory closure. The combination of the disturbing contents, the offhand tone, and the technical deftness of the form makes the poem memorably unsettling.

The last poem (or, perhaps, sequence of poems) in the section, titled "**Small Steps**," is a curious experiment and at times a puzzling one. The poems are in widely different forms and the point of view changes frequently, some sections being written in the second person and some in the first person. The shifts in perspective and the range of forms used seem appropriate since the sequence is essentially a meditation on the fragmentation of identity. The poem records Mason's emergence from a severe bout of depression.

The sequence opens with the instruction, "Open the book of losses," stating that "it begins with early morning light." We pass from a beautiful description of the quiet of early morning, before the house awakes, to the news of a friend on oxygen who "is dying / in a city not so far away." This leads into a section in rhyming dimeter, like a simple nursery rhyme, which evokes the story of Frankenstein's monster. The "lurching creature" remains in the speaker's mind as, in a blank-verse passage, he observes a child learning to walk. It would seem that the sequence is attempting to make some kind of sense of the way we can react to such widely differing experiences—the lives of loved ones ending and other lives beginning around us, the "consolation of the trees" and birdsong. The myth of Frankenstein's monster serves as a correlative for the feeling that we are all "made of past lives brought to life." Similarly, we may feel that the deer, which is described in one of the late sections, as it "flickers across the morning-stippled road / and leaps into shade like a brown trout in a pool," serves as another symbol for the fragmented self, which passes elusively from one experience and one mood to another. In the end, what seems to matter is sensitivity to the varying phenomena of life. "Stop lamenting now, and live," the poem says at one point. Fortunately, it does not end on this somewhat hectoring note, but on a series of unpunctuated observations of the only thing that remains constant in this metamorphic world: change. The last line reads simply:

> *day becomes night becomes day becomes night*

Section 4: Swimmers on the Shore

The final section of the book, "Swimmers on the Shore," takes its title from a poem about the cruelest form of loss of identity, that which is brought about by Alzheimer disease. This is the first of a number of poems that Mason would write on this theme, having observed it firsthand in his mother-in-law and his father. The other poems in the section, even if less anguished, also reflect on the theme of memory, the losses brought about by time and our attempts (mainly doomed) to keep things fixed.

"A Meaning Made of Trees," whose intriguing title comes from a poem in Seamus Heaney's sequence "Crossings," plays on contrasting images of fluidity and solidity. For the liquid sounds, Mason indulges in some splendid Yeatsian alliteration, giving us the "lakewater sounds" of "liquid lapping," the "rain wrung out of the sky," and then, with a gorgeous series of over-the-top consonantal flourishes, he tells us that the alder's leaves "that will fail later in the fall // fulfill themselves, a waterfall / steeped in the greening chlorophyll." Against all this rushing and stirring mellifluousness, he evokes the image of the cedar, which "rises, / huge and straight, the hulking host // and omphalos of my dream world, / its rootedness a kind of triumph."

"The Lost House" offers a metaphor for changes in life, evoking a memory of an adolescent affair of inconclusive sexual fumblings in a half-built house that was later swept away in a landslip: "One night the timbered hillside thundered down / like a dozen freight trains, crashing in a flood / that splintered walls and made the owners run." This catastrophe occurred when the speaker "had been married and divorced." He tells us that "the girl I reached for in unfinished walls / had moved away as if by nature's course." Everything about the story seemed unfinished, even at the time, and now it is as if it had never been. Even the road that once led to the "almost-house" is now

a "dead-end road." The poem is thus a touching tribute to all of life's failures and aborted projects.

"**The Picketwire**" also deals with memory, describing an inevitably unsuccessful attempt to "call back the summer as it stood so still." Of course, the stillness itself was an illusion. The river indicated by the poem's title serves as a perfect symbol for the impossibility of preserving things unchanged. The river was given its name, the poem tells us, by cowboys "because of the way it braided waters tighter," another effective symbol of the illusion of holding things fast. (The poem does not mention this, but the name itself is an indication of the slipperiness of language, since it is in fact a corruption of Purgatoire.) The poem focuses on a sunlit moment from that summer and states, "Remember this, and you are overrun." The final rhyming tercet of the poem offers perfect aural proof of the impossibility of holding on to things:

> A second nature rises from the past,
> just like the first in that it will not last,
> and grips you as it slips free of your grasp.

The witty, consonantal echoes of the opposed words "first" and "last," and then "grips," "slips," and "grasp" in the last line, make the sentence itself sound like a fish wriggling free from one's hands—offering the subliminal suggestion that even the memory of the "fresh-caught trout browning in a pan" might have been an illusion.

"**A Mountain Saxifrage**" also plays on the misleading

notion that names can serve to fix things. In this case, the poet muses on the strikingly odd Latin name of *Boykinia jamesii* for a mountain plant. The plant itself is a perfect symbol of the impermanence of things, being the "cause of the great rock's slow decay." The poem, having fancifully conjured an imaginary boy after whom the plant was named ("Kin to the boy..."), in the final stanza leaves him poised in "A dance in what / was never really there, / a name, a breath of air." At the end, the poem admits the baselessness of the original whimsical invention and with equal capriciousness cancels itself out.

After this indulgence in "airy nothing," "**A Birthday**," written in loose accentual dimeter, begins by evoking a more realistic situation: the poet taking stock at a key point in his life, ten years after Dante's *mezzo del cammin*:

> Dawn of a sort,
> and winter, and I
> am forty-five

But the day doesn't seem to realize its own significance. Everything around him is vague: "dawn of a sort" and "the light indecisive." As if in search of greater precision, he turns "to the published / comfort of maps," where "each thumbprinted mountain" has been "measured, climbed / and claimed ..." This only leads to further musings on the names that have been erased to produce this precision, however: "What is the language / this land would be known by?" Savoring the Spanish names that have survived, he starts a sentence in the optative mood—"If I could hold / this early light …"—and he tries to trawl back through history, all the way to a time "before the Ute / and Comanche at war." The last exotic names he lists, "yucca and yampa," appropriately enough have Native American roots. The sentence concludes with the Adamic wish, "if I could name them / anew the first morning …" But as so often in this book, the sentence is destined never to conclude; he is shaken out of his fruitless musings by the late-twentieth-century sound of a pickup that "grumbles to life." And the poem returns full circle to the opening lines, "as I / become forty-five."

The four poems that follow are all connected with the poet's father, to whom the book is posthumously dedicated. The first, "**Mr Louden and the Antelope**," is a childhood memory of a trip with his father and a one-armed ranching friend, during which they had a sudden vision of antelope, "like dolphins of the desert," that suddenly swept past their truck. Although the vision is the central episode of the poem, what really strikes the reader is the portrait of Mr. Louden, with his humorous acceptance of his disability: "*No, there ain't / nothing funnier than a one-armed man / driving while he tries to swat horseflies.*" By the end of the poem, we are prepared to accept the vision as a dream conjured by this man; even the rust of his battered pickup truck becomes something miraculous in the last line of the poem: "Mr Louden laughed, conjuring with / his only arm, mage of the blooming rust."

The next poem, with the wonderful title "**A Dance in Desolation Sound**," describes a camping expedition undertaken with his father, in search of "mutual solitude." At the heart of this poem, like the sight of antelope in the previous one, is a description of otters playing. The rhyming trimeter stanzas are perfectly attuned to this nocturnal ludic vision:

> Creatures of land and sea,
> their arched, lithe bodies dance.
> They take no notice of me,
> but tumble down the slants
> of rock to moonlit tides,
> then frolic back to the top
> for another of their rides—
> a sort of Otter Hop.

The poet muses on the allegorical significance of this sight, but the poem deliberately avoids forcing an interpretation onto it. Earlier, the poet had imagined that the gulls were mocking him, for his "quixotic notion / that wisdom lies below / in the cold, cold ocean." So he shelves all attempts to go too deeply into matters and returns to his tent: "Whatever this vision meant, / it will have to keep."

"**Winter 1963**" evokes a different moment of communion with his father. It describes witnessing his father's reaction to the news of Robert Frost's death on the car radio; though there is no snow where they are, the announcer's "voice with its calm cadences / lingered by woods where snow fell downily." Mason then inserts his later adult knowledge of the death of Sylvia Plath, just two weeks afterward. He announces his poetic allegiances: "I've tried to cast my lot with that old man, / but something in her fate tugs at me too." The poem finishes on a humble note: "The world goes on despite us and our poems," but nonetheless he feels gratitude for his father's gesture in leaving the radio on. Indeed, since he has told us at the beginning of the poem that the family was coming "home from our rare trip to church," his father's attitude assumes almost religious connotations: "his head / almost bowed as he left the radio on." The poem testifies to the way poetry can touch the lives of nonliterary people.

The last poem on his father in the book, "**Swimmers on the Shore**," is, as already stated, the first of a number that he devotes to his father's illness. Like the later "Father and Sons," this poem focuses on the tragic reversal of roles. He begins with a water image: a memory of playing at the YMCA pool with his father and "diving from his muscled shoulders, / they seemed as solid as two boulders." In the present, the two men are "together / on a park bench in lingering summer weather," and he can hold his father's "shrunken frame / in [his] arm's compass." He sees his father "cast for words," and the simple fishing metaphor heralds the return of water imagery into the poem: "it is as if my father's memories / dissolve in a cedar-darkened pool, / while I no longer am aware / which of us goes fishing there." By the end of the poem, the reversal of familial roles has brought with it also a reversal of metaphorical roles. "There is no doubt, / despite his loss of memory, / and though the words could not be found, / it's I who have begun to drown." The marine imagery has never been more moving.

The next poem serves as coda to the entire volume, summing up all the recurring themes of disorientation and bewilderment, but with a lightness of touch, making ludic use of the imagery of water that has characterized the whole book and engaging in some delicate wordplay. The title itself, "**A Float**," which refers to the object that is the subject of the poem (a Japanese glass float that washed up on a Puget Sound beach and became an ornament in a dead friend's house), could be read as "afloat" and thus alludes to the sensation of bondless drifting that has marked the book so strongly.

Mason opens the poem with two commonly confused words ("Flotsam? Jetsam?"), admitting, with his question marks, to a certain linguistic ignorance. This leads into a series of light word games, where he plays with both the spelling and the sounds of the words: "jet stream," "glass float lost ..." At the heart of the poem is the play on the words "lost" and "found." The poem is not formally rhymed, but these words recur along with a series of consonantal companion words and internal rhymes ("found / on a Puget Sound beach. / The foundling I discovered was not lost // but left ..."). The float becomes a kind of symbol of lostness, as the poet muses on the missing net and the "long-gone fish," and then, like a series of dwindling mirror reflections, on the fisherman, on the "friend / whose house I did not find it in," who is "lost too …" At this point, Mason uses a subtly placed enjambment to jolt us into rethinking what the poem is about. Like many of his poems, it is a reflection on mortality and on what survives us:

> lost too in the sense
> that dead people are
>
> outlasted by a frosty glass ball
> among dog-eared book jackets,
> not bested, not blasted.

He is still playing on the consonantal sounds of the word "lost" ("outlasted," "frosty," "bested," "blasted"), but it is more than just a linguistic game. The last two lines—"Netless, maybe. Uncaught, / unreachable in this room"—return us to the fishing image from the start of the poem but subtly indicate the impossibility of recapturing the essence of a person. It is not too far-fetched to recall his father's gesture, when revisiting the mountains where they had scattered his brother's ashes: "And he waved a hand at the air, signifying where Doug had gone."

The book thus ends with an image of something "uncaught" and "unreachable." But the effect is not dispiriting. The wordplay and the lightness of touch of this poem provide a fittingly buoyant conclusion to a book that is remarkable not only for its geographical breadth but also for its range of tones and its technical mastery. Although dealing with similar themes to those in the two previous volumes, *Arrivals* marks a great advance. After this book, Mason will return to his Colorado roots but with all the confidence of a writer who knows just how far and how deep he can go. Despite its title, *Arrivals* will prove a point of departure. In *Ludlow*, he will transform the optative mood of his birthday poem ("If I could hold / this early light ..."), celebrating the poetry and history of Colorado, into something both commemorative and active.

CHAPTER 6

Ludlow

Ludlow was published in 2007 to general critical acclaim. It won various prizes, including Best Contemporary Poetry Book of the year from *Contemporary Poetry Review*. It is a verse novel of more than 200 pages that recounts the story of the labor disputes in the Colorado coal fields leading up to the massacre of April 20, 1914, at Ludlow, committed by members of the Colorado National Guard against striking miners and their families. Mason tells the story from two perspectives: one is that of a historical figure, Louis Tikas (or Ilias Spantidakis, to give him his real name), a Cretan immigrant who became a union organizer and was killed during the massacre; the other is that of Luisa Mole, a fictional miner's daughter.

The novel comes complete with an impassioned plea (in the afterword) for a return to narrative verse, supported by the voice of Jorge Luis Borges in "The Telling of the Tale":

I believe that the poet shall once again be a maker. I mean, he will tell a story and he will also sing it. And we will not think of those two things as different, even as we do not think they are different in Homer or in Virgil.

One might feel that Mason had already sufficiently made the case for narrative poetry with such works as "The Country I Remember" and "The Collector's Tale." But *Ludlow* is clearly on a different scale of ambition, and concluding his essay with a reference to Homer and Virgil (even if within a quotation) is clearly no accident. *Ludlow*, as Mason has said in a radio interview, is "a small American epic."[1] As if to make his ambitions fully clear, he switches meter for the description of the final battle and uses hexameter—the meter of Homer's epics. Like the *Iliad* and the *Aeneid*, *Ludlow* is about cultural identity. Focusing on a relatively small piece of local history (a "local row," to use Patrick Kavanagh's description of the story behind the *Iliad*, quoted in the author's note to the second edition of *Ludlow*), the work presents the quintessentially American struggle between immigrants and those already established in the land. In a prose interlude in the book, describing his search for the grave of Louis Tikas, the book's protagonist (or hero, why not?), Mason says, "Tikas lies among other immigrants, Polish, Japanese, Hungarian, Italian—all Americans."

Mason is aware of the risks involved in attempting a

---

1. In his foreword to Zeese Papanikolas's book on the Ludlow massacre, Wallace Stegner describes the immigrants' story as "a little Iliad from the losers' side."

long narrative poem on a historical theme. Such works as the *Columbiad* (Joel Barlow, 1807) or *The Mountain Muse* (Daniel Bryan's celebration of Daniel Boone, 1813) are hardly inspiring models. Even *Hiawatha* has become more famous for the parodies it has inspired than for its real virtues (and they exist). In the early decades of the twentieth century, the only full-length narrative poem to tackle the subject of America's greatest historical tragedy in the previous century was the once extremely popular *John Brown's Body* (1928), by Stephen Vincent Benét. This work has almost completely fallen out of public favor, and Mason himself has given a fair assessment of the poem's weaknesses: "It's too devoted to history, too little grounded in character, conflict and scene" ("Narrative Verse," Eratosphere). The historical background in Benét's book is given in sometimes compelling detail, and the historical characters are portrayed with some shrewdness, but the fictional figures in the narrative—Jack Ellyat, of Connecticut, who "thought the thoughts of youth, idle and proud"; Clay Wingate, of Georgia, who "sat in his room at night … /Reading his Byron with knitted brows"; Cudjo the faithful Negro servant and Lucy the Virginia belle—are too much like secondhand copies of characters from *Gone with the Wind*. Mason's comment indicates his ability to learn even from a failure. "Character, conflict and scene" are the qualities that distinguish *Ludlow*.

Nonetheless, Benét's verse novel constituted a valiant attempt to overcome the modernist all but veto on historical narrative. The generation of Pound and Eliot had practically renounced any attempt to present history as *story*.[2] Although Pound's *Cantos* are steeped in a profound if idiosyncratic awareness of historical matters, the poet makes no endeavor to present the events of history in narrative or even in anecdotal form. The reader must either be already acquainted with the facts to which reference is made or attempt to re-create the story from the gobbets and nuggets that are dropped in enticing but frustratingly incomplete fashion onto the page.

Benét was not the only poet of the generation after Pound and Eliot to attempt to tackle historical themes, but he was perhaps unique in his blithe refusal to take into any account the modernist legacy. Such poets as Robert Penn Warren, John Berryman, and Robert Lowell all showed their awareness of modernist methods in such works as *Brother to Dragons* (1953) and *Audubon: A Vision* (1969), *Homage to Mistress Bradstreet* (1953), and the sonnets of *History* (1973). This last work is perhaps the most ambitious, an attempt by Lowell to present the entire history of humanity in a sequence of 368 sonnets; from his modernist forebears Lowell had certainly learned the technique of concentration. The dazzling detail—the "flash-in-the-pan" invoked in the very first sonnet—seems to have been what Lowell had in mind, and amid the confusing pleth-

2. The best account of the treatment of historical themes in American poetry from modernism onward is Robert B. Shaw's essay "Contrived Corridors" in *The Contemporary Narrative Poem: Critical Crosscurrents* (ed. Steven P. Schneider), to which I am indebted.

ora of names, such images provide occasional moments of startling illumination, but all too often the compression is so intense as to provoke mere bewilderment. The overall impression is that we are being allowed a glimpse of the writer's random desk jottings.

It was not until the 1980s that historical verse narrative made a decided comeback. Although narrative poetry in itself had never gone away (Frost, Jeffers and Robinson proved that, as did the later generation of Hecht and Simpson), it was only with the "broad resurgence of interest in narrative and dramatic verse" (Afterword, *Ludlow*) of Mason's own generation that a significant number of large-scale works were published on historical themes. Examples were Daniel Hoffman's *Brotherly Love* (1981), Andrew Hudgins's *After the Lost War* (1988), Mason's own "The Country I Remember" (1996), Mary Jo Salter's "The Hand of Thomas Jefferson" (1994), William Jay Smith's *The Cherokee Lottery* (2000), and Marilyn Nelson's *Carver: A Life in Poems* (2001). *Ludlow* therefore does not come out of the blue. What does distinguish Mason's work is the continued emphasis on the importance of making a story out of the facts: "These are the facts, but facts are not the story." To a certain extent, one could say that *Ludlow* is also *about* making a story out of history.

In the author's note to the second edition, he states, "In writing my version I have concerned myself less with verifiable facts than with the weight of imagined lives and the lyrical nature of stories." The novel is "a work of fiction, a dreamscape and not a documentary." Elsewhere he states that what he is after is "the ground sense of the thing, the experience of being in the skin of a person" (*Able Muse*, 139). There is no doubt that the reason *Ludlow* is such a compelling work is that Mason succeeds in entering the skins of his two main characters, Louis Tikas and Luisa Mole. He can tell their stories because they are partly his.

Both characters are displaced persons, with allegiances to different worlds, and both are trying to establish a sense of identity and belonging. In his author's note, Mason states, "I wrote *Ludlow* partly to root myself back in the West after twenty years of wandering." Mason is rediscovering—but also reconsidering—those roots. In the story, he makes use of his family background; as he says in his afterword, "the voices of my grandfather Abraham and his four sons still sound in my head." His great-grandfather (whom he never met) had one of the notorious pluck-me stores, before opening a more legitimate business in Trinidad.

The story is told for the most part in the third person, something he had only done before in the poem "The Escape." But he himself frequently intervenes in the narration, admitting frankly that the "story's partly mine." His first intervention comes with the words "I know that sky," leading two lines later to the statement, "I have come back." What follows is a childhood memory:

> I first saw this land in a boyhood dream
> made of my father's stories. Colorado,

where the red of earth turned at night to the blue
of moonlit heaven, where coyotes yapped
up the arroyo, and the deer came down
to seek unsullied water in the streams.
It was a fantasy:
cowboys and Indians. *Home on the Range.*

The unreality of this, emphasized by the comic placing
of the exotic words ("where coyotes yapped / up the arroyo"), does not actually undermine its evocative power. If
it doesn't evoke the reality, it evokes at least the dream—
and thus testifies to the power of his father's stories. Mason makes it clear how important such stories are in our
apprehension of a land. In the final chapter, Luisa runs off
with Lefty Calabrini, one of her father's workmates, and
they board a train that takes them to "New Mexico, / her
mother-country, land she'd never seen / except in stories
that her parents told." So she, too, presumably had her
own dream of her mother's homeland, one based on stories told her as a child. At the end of the novel, as an old
woman, she falls in with hippies who have set up a com-
mune just outside Trinidad; she "tells them stories of the
mines / and how this land was full of immigrants / who
fought and lost, and most have moved away." She realizes
as she speaks, however, that "it isn't history they want / but
present life, each instant a new session / cut off from the
past, alive until spent, / young desert swimmers trying to
stay uncaught / by ordinary nets."

This realization, which ties in with Mason's opinions

expressed elsewhere on the historical and cultural amnesia of Americans, leads into the conclusion and the climax of the novel. At this moment, Luisa does not give up the task of communicating with these people. She knows she has nothing "but her own stories" to give them. Turning a tiny stone in her hand, which serves as a kind of bond to the land where her people lie "beneath hardscrabble surfaces," she "gather[s]" her story and prepares to tell it anew. In these final stanzas, the blank-verse stanzas have taken on rhyme and the voice has become more lyrical:

> I dream of Luisa gathering her story,
> no trace of her parents' accent left in her,
> though they are part of her life's inventory.
> She uses names like Tikas, Rockefeller,
> Lawson, Mother Jones. The communards
> have heard of some of these, and she unveils
> a vision of the camps in simple words,
> a scrap of song, a memory of hills.

Paradoxical though it might seem to say so, after more than 200 pages of mainly blank-verse narrative, this is ultimately the ambition of the book: to communicate such a vision, to leave behind a memory of hills. Mason has chosen to tell his story in verse precisely so that these names— together with the fictional but representative names of Luisa and Too Tall Macintosh, the Reeds and Lefty Calabrini and others—will not be forgotten. This is the poet's job, to leave behind "a scrap of song" so that things shall be remembered.

The phrase "part of her life's inventory" had been used earlier by the poet with reference to himself, in the first "Interlude," at the beginning of Part Two: "My ancestors were business folk who ran / a pluck me store. [...] Their lives are part of my life's inventory; / my role grows smaller when I glimpse the whole. / Today I pocketed a lump of coal. / These are the facts, but facts are not the story." Seeing one's ancestors as part of one's life's inventory means taking stock of the importance of one's roots, setting oneself within a larger framework. It is an act of humility and involves repositioning oneself—also with regard to the earth itself. Just as Luisa does with the small stone at the end of the novel, Mason picks up a lump of coal, as if to anchor himself to the hard things of the earth. They are, after all, an essential part of the story.

The line "These are the facts, but facts are not the story" also recurs in the novel; it appears as the opening line of chapter 10, immediately after the first battle:

> These are the facts, but facts are not the story ...
> There was a weight, a person with a name.
> That weight is gone, in ashes or in earth.

Musing on mortality and on "glory," Mason then describes a visit to a bookshop: "The facts, the facts. I buy a battered book / about the massacre at Ludlow, and the man / who sells it to me asks a modest price ..." Apparently suspicious of the political line Mason is likely to take, the man tells him "with a heavy look" that "the whole thing got out of

hand" and "It wasn't a massacre of the innocents."[3] Mason
assures him that he is not intending to judge, but

> [I] fail to mention what I dream of writing:
> a tale in verse about the immigrants,
> the pluck me stores, the dodge
> of truth among arroyos where the fighting
> razed all hope of prospering, and the fenced
> land hardened and the people went away
> and died as surely as they lived a day.

In essence, what he fails to mention to the man is that he
dreams of making it a story. In the afterword, Mason con-
siders the question of how one can sustain lyrical intensity in a book-length narrative and acknowledges that Poe
had a point when he claimed that "the quotient of poetry
would be diminished the longer the poet kept going." He
adds, however, "lyric intensity is not the only component
of a good narrative poem. There is also the story, and if you
have a good one it will have a form of its own. To me, the
story is a remarkable and irreducible element of humanity." This is an essential statement, one that throws light on
all of Mason's works.

Mason acknowledges the debt he owes to those who
have gathered the facts, in particular, Zeese Papanikolas,
the biographer of Louis Tikas, who "heard the rambling

3. It is worth pointing out that Mason is never simplistic in his presentation of
the events. He does not hide the fact that the miners themselves were responsible
for a good deal of violence. He gives fair and rounded portraits of such figures as
John D. Rockefeller.

men / who patched their memories, stitching the rags / of hearsay, myth, and resurrected desire." Admitting that "we piece together Tikas," he declares his own contribution to the legend-making:

> Imagination's arrogance is all
> I bring to this, a storyteller's hope
> of touching life in others, a poet's love
> of tropes and cadences, the sway of words.

He follows this declaration by indicating just why he feels particularly suited to the task of "piecing together" Tikas:

> Because this story hooks into desires
> I've always felt to know the land I come from,
> Tikas is one figure I summon back.
> Because I lived in Greece, I once reversed
> his journey, hoped to find my life abroad
> and failed, though not for any lack of love,
> I know the salt and brilliance of his sea,
> the heat that stuns you, the cicadas' whir,
>
> the bite of ráki on a lover's tongue.

This passage makes it clear just how important the sense of place is in giving life to these characters. He can "summon back" Tikas by drawing on his own experience of the land of Greece. And as the last line here reveals, Greece is a sensual experience before it is an intellectual one.

We are first introduced to Tikas in chapter 4, whose title "The Greek-American" at once underlines his hyphenated identity. The opening line gives us his Greek name,

Ilias Spantidakis, and in the second stanza, we learn that he does not in fact feel Greek but Cretan. He thus appears to be characterized by a whole series of internal divisions:

> Some days this waking to himself became
> unbearable, like some ill-fitting task,
> the words he'd learned of English hard to hold,
> his village dialect a refuge from
> estranging streets. How long, O Lord, how long
> must one man journey till he finds his home?

This sense of a divided self—a man with a new name, new country, new identity but old yearnings—is crucial. The chapter shows us how the man's inner life and dreams do not correspond to his public life and image. Mason has said in interviews that he feels close to Tikas; one could say that with the character of Tikas he continues his exploration of the mysteries of the fragmented identity, already seen in such poems as "Small Steps."

Some of the most moving passages in the book draw on Tikas's yearnings for and memories of Crete:

> For all the years he'd lived in America
> he'd felt the torture of its emptiness.
> The quiet of a village just at nightfall,
> goat bells, women's voices, rustle of leaves,
> came back as steadily as waves, as wind
> in olive branches he had climbed as a boy
> to feel them swaying like small boats at sea.
> He felt that constant sway and almost cried.

This stanza comes after a highly effective description of Tikas's first experiences in a mine, where the emphasis is on the noise, the intensity of the work, the filth, and the claustrophobia: "all within / the bustling, pounding, smoky, hacking compound / where generators whined, electric lights / on long wires flickered in the gloom." Mason brilliantly creates a sense of the inhuman, mechanical nature of this world and its sounds and sights: "an elevator / scraped its stanchion, agonies of steel / that echoed up the shaft." By contrast, Crete in Tikas's memories appears to be a hushed world, where the sounds of life are all natural and gentle. Mason may be drawing, perhaps unconsciously, on a description of Tikas that is given in Papanikolas's book; the union leader John Lawson talked of him as "one of the quietest men he ever knew" (91). (We know that this is a partial view of Crete, since Tikas has other vivid memories of civil war on the island, but no one is all-encompassing when indulging in nostalgia.)

The marine imagery in this evocative passage is also important, serving as another obvious point of contrast with Colorado. Even the olive trees, it seems, remind one that Crete is an island. In a later passage, the contrast is made even more evident:

> Tikas, awake, surprised to feel such grief,
> tasted the salt of tears that came in dreams
> and knew what he had missed was almost freedom,
> years ago in sunlight when he drank
> the virgin pressing of the oil like wine

at his father's house. Oh God, he missed the sea,
the tears of an eternity of men,
the peacefulness of swimming under water.

He missed the smell of grass in autumn rain,
the sacks of dripping goat cheese hung from rafters,
the words like *thálassa* and *ouranós*
that felt to him much weightier than English.

Crete, despite the dry heat of its summers, is here evoked in a series of images that all suggest moistness and liquidity. This is emphasized by repeated "s" sounds, many of them double ("missed," "pressing," "peacefulness," "grass," "*thálassa*"). From oil we pass to wine, and then, perhaps by Homeric association, to the sea, and thence to wet grass and dripping goat cheeses. Coming straight after the goat cheeses, the two Greek words, chosen partly for the contrast with the brevity of the corresponding English words (sea and sky), are made to seem not only weightier but also more sensuous; we can taste and smell these words, unlike the "cardboard words" of American.

When writing of Colorado, the emphasis is continually on aridity. This is the case even in the early description, which draws on Mason's childhood dreams of the place:

A solitary cone of rock rose up
from lacerated land, the dry arroyos,
scars that scuppered water in flood season
down to a river. In dusty summertime
the cottonwoods eked out a living there

in a ragged line below the high peaks.
The ground was a plate of stony scutes that shone
like diamonds at noon, an hour when diamondbacks

coiled on sunbaked rocks. Or so I pictured
in color films imagination shot.

This is one of Mason's virtuoso passages and scarcely needs
comment. One might just point to the brilliant choice of
"scutes"—the plated scales of a tortoise—which works
both aurally, continuing the series of strong "sc-" sounds,
and semantically, suggesting hardness and dryness, and
leads by association to the image of the diamondback
snake.

As the last lines make clear, this description is still con-
ditioned by the child's imagination. In a later description
of a visit to the mesa country in search of arrowheads with
his grandfather, he gives us another, more "realistic" impression of the land. The emphasis is still on dryness:

Windblown aridity in early spring,
piñon, prickly pear, the struggling scrub.
At noon my shadow pooled beneath my boots,
my eyes surveying ground a step ahead
for arrowheads or any signs of life,
out walking a friend's ranch with Abraham,
the land a maze of dry arroyos, slabs
of pale rock, the flints exposed by weather.

To bring home the full bleakness of this picture, he describes
how he stumbled into a ditch "and fell across the corpse /

of a calf the wild coyotes dined upon, / a gutted leathery thing—it had a face ..." The shock of this is exacerbated by the bareness of the vocabulary; the vagueness ("leathery thing," "a face") is far more effective than a detailed description of the gruesome features would have been.

The corpse is one of the "terrible remains of winter." There are moments when the climate seems to be another major character in the story. The descriptions of Colorado winter are memorably bleak:

> At the first corpse-colored light on snowy ground
> the men were up and moving, stomping boots
> and swinging arms to pump blood into them.

He takes a small event that occupied three lines in Papanikolas's book—"In the Trinidad jail sleet drifted through the broken windows. Tikas and the fifteen other prisoners of Chase's army slept on bunks covered with three inches of snow" (136)—and turns it into this:

> He almost sniffed the change of weather, light
> on the bars like dusk. The walls dropped water
> and his breath steamed, and the broth they served at noon
> turned quickly cold.
> And one night in December snow flew in,
> blanketing his blanket until he woke
> and watched the little streetlit flakes of silver
> float into the dark above his head.
>
> He reached, and snow lay several inches deep
> on his wet blanket, spilling on the floor,

and cellmates stirred, cursing this circumstance
and cursing just to keep their faces warm.

It is, in short, a hard land, summer and winter. It is hard in
every sense of the word. One could say that its hardness
has been a constant theme from the very beginning of the
novel. The opening lines indicate the violent means that
are necessary to obtain a living from this soil:

Shot-firers filed in after the diggers left
and found the marked drills for their measured shot.
As daylight died the men were blasting deep
for the next day's cuts of coal.

Mason uses the technique of full and instant immersion: we are at once thrust into an impersonal world of
regimented work, with no explanation of its terminology
being offered and no faces or names given. The anonymous
workers live in a permanent nocturnal atmosphere, passing
"from dark / to dark below, / from desert stars to flickering
kerosene." The cabins where they live above ground are a
"twilit Babel," amid which Luisa scrubs pots and hauls water. She is the first person to be named and described, if
but sketchily: "scrawny, barely twelve." The violence of her
world is made brutally clear to us in an updated version of
the Homeric simile, describing how the noises of the ex-
plosions below ground reach Luisa: "dull thudding sounds
/ like the push of air a man's torso made / when other men
lit into him with fists. / The mesa sounded like a beaten
man, // pinned down and beaten senseless in the night."

We are not therefore surprised by the violent reaction of Luisa to the news of her father's death: "There was the girl, of course, who ran out screaming / when she heard, and seemed to pummel the earth, / her fists stuck full of cactus spines and bleeding ..." Just as the earth punished her, so she hysterically attempts to punish it back; of course, it is the well-armored earth that comes off best.

Our next picture of the girl comes after one of the novel's more striking descriptive passages, which deliberately echoes Whitman:

> Out of the rockfolds, the scrub, the deep sky,
> out of the junipers that loosed the dark
> when the sun crept over the mountaintops,
> out of the mouths and tipples of the mines
> where men still worked, inquest or no inquest,
> where coke ovens glowed a stone inferno,
> out of the train that wailed to Trinidad
> and back to Denver with its load of news
>
> came the sound that was not a sound, a muted
> scratching for life.

Whereas the corresponding passage in Whitman's "Out of the Cradle" concludes with the poet raising his own voice ("I, chanter of pains and joys [...] a reminiscence sing"), in Mason's passage, after the cinematic overview of the land, the mountains, and the unrelenting work of men, we reach the dry scratching of the hens that Luisa has been put in charge of. She assigns names and personalities to these birds, which, like her, attempt to scratch a living from the arid earth, but she also witnesses their inevitable end: "She watched as a woman scooped up a hen / by the legs, stepped on its squawking head, and jerked."

The story will be partly her story: we see her being removed from the community and sent to town to work for a middle-class family, and then we get glimpses of her life, torn between this well-meaning but frustratingly close-knit family and the mining world. While working for the Reed family, she recounts stories of her earlier life to the little boy, Pud: "He listened when she told of mining camps / where everybody had a funny name / and blew things up, or so it seemed." An encounter in the Reeds' shop with an old friend of her father's, Too Tall Macintosh (one of the most attractive characters in the novel), leaves her feeling "[t]orn in two // by what she saw both far and near, outside / herself and deep inside [...] Luisa knew that something of herself / was gypsy and untouchable and never / to be saved." When she goes with another old acquaintance, Lefty Calabrini, to hear Mother Jones, the leftwing agitator, the family is shocked. George Reed, whom she had admired till that moment, dismisses Mother Jones ("as nutty as a fruitcake"), and Luisa finds herself resisting him:

> Luisa heard from far away, as if
> an ice age had moved in from western peaks
> along the Purgatoire, as if her mind
> flew backwards like a frightened bird and found
> the slag and filth of childhood and her skin
> rebelled and stood its ground and would not hear.

The curious thing about this passage is that even her rejection of George Reed is presented as a divided experience, her mind and her skin pulling her in different directions. Eventually, she will reconcile the urges of both skin and mind, standing her ground on behalf of the crude, rough world (the "slag and filth") of her childhood. She joins the women's march in support of Mother Jones and the miners. Mason makes Luisa the girl at whom General Chase, at the head of the National Guard, absurdly swung his sword (an actual event, reported in Papanikolas's book). As a result, Luisa ends up in jail with the other women. From this point on, her allegiance to the miners and their cause will know no wavering.

One can presume that Mason gave Luisa a similar name to the novel's other main character in order to suggest that their fates are intertwined. The gradual converging of their two destinies is one of the ways he structures the story, even though the two of them barely meet.[4] The convergence is toward the killing field of Ludlow, rather than toward a personal encounter. Also in Louis Tikas's case we get the impression of a kind of irresistible force propelling him toward his final and fatal encounter. His standoffs with the brutal Karl Linderfelt ("Someday"—"Let her come"—another episode mentioned in Papanikolas's book) contribute to this sense of impending doom.

Momentum gathers in the second half of the book, and

4. In the libretto for the operatic version of the novel, Mason has created a love story between the two characters, with a duet that they sing while in prison.

Mason marks the passing of time by descriptions of the seasons and references to the religious feasts. He adapts a Christmas carol to his purpose:

> *God rest ye merry, gentlemen.*
> *Let nothing ye dismay.*
> *Remember Christ, our savior*
>   *was born on Christmas day.*
> But nothing was the word of peace.
>   Nothing would offer love.
> Nothing would give the world release
>   from the nothing of God above.

The final battle—"the hardest day of all to write about"—takes place instead "with Greeks still celebrating Christ / alive in the blue dome of Heaven." It is a compellingly written chapter; the switch to hexameter confers a sense of added urgency. As we have seen, Luisa has returned to her childhood roots. In a tragic way, something similar seems to be true of Louis Tikas at the height of the battle:

> Brute force had won. Brute force controlled the
>   heavens now.

> The light almost the light of Greece without a sea,
> as if a million years had passed since early morning
> and he was older now, much more than twenty-eight,
> and this was Crete without salt water, the warrior dance
> of villagers. Slabs of piney desert, thorns
> and stones and sacrifice and endless killing rage.
> He'd never crossed the ocean. This was a bad dream.
> No—a bullet fell nearby, and it was real.

"Greece without a sea" is practically an oxymoron. But at the same time, one could say that it is at this crucial point that Tikas recalls another side to his homeland: Crete is not just a land of goat bells, swaying olive trees, and dripping cheeses. Chapter 4, in which we were introduced to Tikas, opened with the lines "Ilias Spantidakis lay awake / in the narrow bed behind his *kafeneion* / thinking of gunfire." These early passages evoke the brutal civil war on the island between Turks and Greeks. Colorado, despite the absence of salt water, is not necessarily so very different. Tikas has come home—and we remember the lines that concluded chapter 4, "The Greek American":

> A story is the language of desire.
> A journey home is never what it ought
> to be.
> > A land of broken glass. Of gunfire.

Tikas's death—the ultimate journey home—is followed by the second prose interlude, dated January 16, 2003. This takes the shape of a series of short paragraphs, their disconnected appearance on the page reflecting the turmoil in the narrator's mind as he wonders if he "could ever pull together [his] own version" of the "collage of voices in Papanikolas's book." He writes in a motel, the perfect symbol of rootless modern America, throwing pages on the floor and rewriting them as he asks himself, "What are we to do? We, the ungrounded ones?" He then pays a visit to those who are grounded in every sense of the word: the dead in the cemetery of Trinidad. He observes the new pink granite slab erected for Tikas and its elaborate inscription, ending with the single word "PATRIOT."

Just seventy-five yards to the north and east lie Mason's own grandparents. And so the principal strands of the story—the personal story and the public history—are drawn together; Mason even reflects that Tikas died at the same age as his brother, Doug. There are stones for his grandparents and for Louis Tikas, but "no stone for Luisa Mole, none for the Reeds, so many others." What follows is the justification of his fictionalization of history, of his making a story out of history: "I write for them as well. And I write, as they say, for myself. I write of them to feel more alive in my own skin, as if my existence were finally as real as theirs."

In the last paragraph, Mason depicts his own journey home from Trinidad, listing the place names. He concludes with one last significant name: "On the way home I would take the freeway exit and the gravel road out to *El huerfano*, a moonscape in these days of drought, and stand there for a long while with the orphan, as if it might whisper its stony secret in my ear."[5] The two concluding verse chapters that follow the interlude are divided between the public history, providing a list of the recorded victims of the massacre and describing the post-massacre lives of the survivors, and the private story of Luisa Mole, known

5. *El huerfano*, or "The Orphan," is an isolated volcanic neck in southern Colorado.

throughout the novel as *la huerfana*. The title of the final chapter is "A Stone for Luisa Mole." We have already seen how Luisa, before telling her story to the hippie community, picks up a tiny stone, which serves as a bond to the land and to the people who have gone before her. The title indicates how this chapter—and indeed the whole novel—constitutes the memorial stone he has chosen to erect to these people. It is fitting that the stone Luisa handles is a small one, which she can turn in a ritualistic, even thaumaturgic fashion. Mason's own memorial is impressive but never ponderous, and for all its tragic import ultimately convinces us of its healing powers.

CHAPTER 7

Sea Salt

Mason's fifth full-length poetry book, *Sea Salt*, came out in 2014, bearing the subtitle *Poems of a Decade, 2004–2014*. The poems chronicle a crucial ten-year period of his life, during which one marriage failed and a new life began. There are poems that testify to periods of intense loneliness and anguish ("The Tarmac"), as well as poems that confess movingly to deception ("The Man Who Lied") and to the pain that came with separation ("Child," "Prayer to the Air"). These poems are among the most moving he has written. And there are the passionate and joyous lyrics that celebrate his newfound love. The volume also contains moving poems that focus on his parents, inspired by the painful experience of his father's dementia and his mother's death. Memory plays a more crucial role than ever, as he recollects his childhood and his youthful travels, recollections in part inspired by a return to certain significant locations in Greece.

The volume opens with a lyric in rhyming quatrains

that has a distinctly Greek word as title: "*Kéfi.*" Numerous webpages on Greek culture state that this word, although usually translated as "a spirit of joy," in fact refers to a key element in Greek life and culture, and it is actually untranslatable. In *News from the Village*, Mason describes it as "one of the ineffable pleasures of life." This poem, which serves as gateway to the whole book, opens with rather unsettling words: "Every meal a communion. / The uninvited dead are here." But by the third stanza, the speaker describes himself as "Light-headed in this company" and explicitly states that "The Greeks would call this *kéfi,* // ineffable, weightless, tuned / to the conversations of the night / with or without a moon."

This communion with the dead points to what will be a recurring theme in the book: the commemoration of deceased acquaintances, friends, and relatives. As the final stanza indicates, however, this will not necessarily be a melancholy process:

> It's *kéfi*—coffee would wreck it,
> or too much wine, but a song
> if I can remember it
> will carry us along.

The near pun on "*kéfi*—coffee" keeps the tone light, as the speaker invokes what will turn out to be the book's tutelary spirit: that of song. The words "if I can remember it" gesture to the role that memory will play throughout.

The book is divided into three numbered but untitled

sections. The middle one (the longest) is preceded by two epigraphs, while the first and last are distinguished only by their numbers. All the sections contain a wide range of poetic forms and themes so that the rationale behind the division is not immediately clear. The first section can perhaps be distinguished from the other two in a negative sense, as it contains no love poems. For the most part, the poems in this section dwell on family concerns or childhood memories.

The second poem in the section, "**New World**," depicts a mysterious but distinctly American landscape, as the title would suggest. The opening image, "Snow in the pines, spring snow," suggests both endings and beginnings, a notion given greater force, if not clarity, in lines three and four: "The felled trees lie in the steaming forest / lit by the far coals of the world's beginning." The next line introduces an image that will recur in each section of the book, that of an elusive fox: "The fox darts over jeweled kinnikinnik—" This last word, of Proto-Algonquian origin, refers to a compound of bark and leaves, used as an herbal smoking mixture, and thereby connected with the realm of the hallucinatory, or at least the oneiric. The fox, as we will see most significantly in the final poem of the second section, would seem to be associated with poetic inspiration. For the moment, the speaker can only aspire to follow the swift movements of the animal (*"Be quick, be quick,"* urges the speaker, perhaps spurred by the sounds of the preceding Native American word), in the hope of "another chance at waking."

The third poem, "**A Thorn in the Paw**," is a reflection on religion—or, rather, on the speaker's lack of religious belief. Paradoxically, he uses a highly charged allegorical conceit to make his point, of the kind traditionally associated with devotional poetry, identifying his godless condition with that of "a young dog with a big thorn / in its paw, becoming that very thorn." It is a curiously powerful poem, testifying to a sense of loss, or at least exile, as the speaker feels cut off from others who "grew up with chrism, incense, law" and who "had pews and prayer-shawls, old fathers / telling them when to kneel and what to say." The most beautiful lines in the poem describe the natural world:

> Birds high up in their summer baldachin
> obey the messages of wind and leaves.
> Their airy hosannas
> can build a whole day out of worming and song.

Even as he describes their self-sufficiency (with envy?), he finds himself forced to use imagery taken from the world of religious ceremony or devotion. The poem concludes with the speaker's declaration, "Nobody gave me a god / so I perfect my idolatry of doubt."

In the next two poems, Mason returns to narrative. "**The Teller**" is a highly compressed tale (it is one of two sonnets in the volume), which works perhaps more as a reflection on narrative than as a narrative per se. It tells, in tightly rhyming lines, the story of a "rawboned Eskimo named Jack" and his five-year involuntary exile. The story raises more questions than it answers, starting with the name of the protagonist, which turns out to have been given to him by "an Englishman." The final sestet of the sonnet plays on the word "name," slant-rhyming it with the place names "Nam" and "Nome," this last Alaskan toponym rhyming fully with the earlier "home" of line eight—but also anticipating the final words of the poem, in which the speaker confesses the unreliable nature of the story: "The man who told me? I tell you, I don't know." Even as he uses the clichéd expression supposed to guarantee authenticity ("I tell you"), he admits to its fallibility.

However, the narrative that follows, "The Fawn," appears to be a full return to the narrative mode for which Mason is best known. It tells a story from childhood, recounting how a visiting cousin, Maren, attempted to save the life of a fawn that had been mangled by a neighbor's dog. The story is told in convincing detail, paying tribute to the devoted care of the young girl, who nursed the sick animal, until a week later the speaker's "father backed the car to the garage / to carry out the dead fawn in a tarp / and bury it in some deep part of the woods, / unmarked, and later unremarked upon / with summer over and our cousin gone." It is the postscript to the story that carries the greatest weight. In a few lines, Mason packs in "a world of change" that befell both the family and the nation after 1963 or 1962, whichever it was (and the speaker's uncertainty recalls the famous dithering over Fredericksburg or

Gettysburg in Frost's "Black Cottage"): "I know / it was before the war divided us / and more than that, before our parents grew / apart like two completely different species …" Maren, we are told, became "a rancher's wife / in Colorado, she was all for Jesus […] We gave up calling and we never write." In five lines, Mason recounts how his parents' lives fell to pieces after his brother's death before saying, "The years are a great winnowing of lives, / but we had knelt together by the fawn …" The final lines read:

> I'm still there, looking at that dying fawn,
> at how a girl's devotion almost saved it,
> wet panic in its eyes, its shivering breath,
> its wild heart beating on the concrete floor.

Without forcing things, he allows the reader to see an analogy between the desperate frailty of the animal and the lost innocence of both the family and the nation. This moment of shared compassion did not save the animal, but it remains an indelible memory for the writer. The last line, with its simultaneous evocation of wildness and the products of an industrial society, recalls the concluding lines of Elizabeth Bishop's poem "The Moose": "then there's a dim / smell of moose, an acrid / smell of gasoline." The poem is also a reflection on our relationship with the natural world.

His father is present in the next four poems. In "**Lieutenant Mason**," he returns to his father's wartime experiences, as in "A Textbook of Navigation and Nautical

Astronomy" in his first book. This time, however, he explicitly describes the horrors that his father witnessed while patrolling the waters of Iwo Jima. He has recounted the story in the title essay of *The Poetry of Life*, where he states, "The memory of dead and wounded boys has never left my father; it may have contributed to his decision after the war to become a doctor. He could not talk about it for years." In the poem "Lieutenant Mason," he opens with a shocking image: "You have to stuff it all back in, / the gut from a nicked / peritoneum." The poem continues with a series of equally graphic images; the phrase "You have to put it back" is repeated, as a symbol of the need for the mind to repress such memories: "That's how a lifetime passes, / closing, re-closing the wound ..." But after a series of images centered on the notion of tight closure, through knots and stitches, the poem concludes with a series of lines that become progressively shorter while paradoxically expressing a final acceptance of the need to open oneself:

> until you learn to let
> it lie and let
> it weep,
> and open.

This poem is followed by "**Energy**," avowedly about an old friend of his father's, but also about his brother's death. The energy of the title is evoked by the family friend as an explanation for where the brother had gone: "*It's energy*, /

you said. *That energy must still be somewhere.*" The poet undertakes to carry out the task that the friend feels inadequate to ("*I've seen so many things,* you said. *I wish / I could write them down*"), declaring in the final lines that he "will try / to catch the light, the flavor of the air / Like moss, like distant ice, like clear water." These are indeed the elements that in his earlier poems have been clearly associated with his mountaineering brother, and they are beautifully captured in this tender and touching evocation of a solicitous friend.

The next two poems deal with his father's Alzheimer disease. One of them, published in the *New Yorker* in September 2009, is titled simply "**Fathers and Sons.**" It attempts to disarm criticism right away by stating, "Some things, they say, / one should not write about," and then proceeds to recount how the son had to help his "father comprehend / the toilet." Reacting to the son's laughter, his father gripped him, "trembling, searching for my eyes. / *Don't you*—but the word / was lost to him. Somewhere / a man of dignity would not be laughed at." The poem ends by fully restoring the father's dignity to him, as the poet declares that it was "the crazy dance / that made me laugh, / trying to make him sit / when he wanted to stand." It is a wonderful tribute to the indomitable self-respect of a man who has lost all else.

The other poem, "**Home Care,**" begins with a surreal statement from his father: "My father says his feet will soon be trees ..." It recounts a visit to the home where his father now lives and the subsequent trip outside, with his father "regressed at eighty-two / to mooncalf prominence, drugged and adrift." The final two lines sadly give point to his father's strange declaration, as the poet muses, "He will be ashes in a summer shower / and sink to roots beneath the winter's weight."

The penultimate poem in this section, **"Mrs. Vitt,"** is a moving tribute in blank verse to the poet's teacher in his second grade: "The first to realize what a liar I was." The narrator describes visiting his former teacher at her home, after she had retired because of Parkinson's disease. The steady iambic pulse of the lines acts as melancholy counterpoint to the highly effective description he gives of the woman's uncontrollable shaking:

> It took her husband many lighter flicks
> to catch her swaying cigarette.

The final line of the poem, delivered by Mrs. Vitt after the speaker has apologized for the "grief" he must have given her with his lies, is moving in its simplicity:

> And she, with each word shuddered out in smoke:
> *No child I taught was any grief to me.*

The last poem in the section, **"Driving with Marli,"** remains within the ambit of the family and is closely linked in theme to the opening lyric of the second section, "Child." In both poems we see the poet dealing with the repercussions of his failed marriage on his relations with a younger generation. They testify to inner anguish and guilt, combined with a sense of loss and displacement. In "Driving with Marli," an irregularly rhyming poem, the poet attempts to answer the naive question of a 3-year-old child (*"Grandpa, do you live in the sky?"*) with an honest and realistic answer ("No, but I live on a mountain / and came on a plane to see you"). The second stanza, however, after some wry interior debates, ends with a frank admission, in suitably nursery-rhyme-like language: "I do live in the sky, / but I do not know why." This simple but moving declaration of helplessness concludes the book's first section.

The sense of disorientation is taken up in the two epigraphs to the next section, the first from the metaphysical poet Thomas Stanley: "Waters, plants and stones know this, / That they love, not what love is," and the second from John Keats's letters: "Call the world if you please 'The vale of Soul-making.' Then you will find out the use of the world …" There are a number of fine love poems in this section, but even as they declare their passion, they also express a sense of awed wonder at the mystery of it. The great upheaval in Mason's personal life brought about by this new love perhaps explains the epigraph from Keats, as he seeks, amid emotional turmoil, to "find out the use of the world."

As already indicated, the first poem, "**Child**," is connected with the last of the previous section, expressing as it does a sense of sorrow at the sadness caused by the change in familial relations. The central metaphor of this short lyric is that of uncontrollable tidal currents, and it concludes, "My flesh is feeling clay / eroded by more tides than I can blame / or bring myself to name." Sea imagery will permeate the remaining poems in the volume, often associated with his new love.

The three poems that follow are bewildering in their widely diverse subject matters and emotions, ranging from the tender recollective note of "**The Nape**" ("I brushed my lips on her skin / and felt her present through me / there in the cidery light") to the yearning tones of "**The Future**" ("Like you I am trying / to leave my luggage / behind in the car / or the circling carousel …") and the unsettling shrillness of "**The Wards**," with its sharp but fragmentary images of madness and despair ("They nurse their lurid sores / and suck from paper bags"); this last poem seems to echo "The Escape" in *The Country I Remember*. The only unifying factor is a sense of disruption, with vivid if sometimes confusing glimpses of another life—either yearned for or rejected.

The short poem "**The Man Who Lied**," with its sharp accentual tetrameter and vigorous rhymes, conveys the sense of fraught agitation of a life given over to deception. The poem ends with two questions—"why all the running? When will it end?"—which suggest that deception is an irrepressible compulsion ("an inner eel"), whose effects are as devastating on the perpetrator as on his victims, reducing him to a "Scab man, scar man, scolding himself."

Images of trauma are also found in a mysterious short narrative poem, **"In the Barber Shop,"** which describes, in four six-line stanzas in blank verse, an episode witnessed in a barber's shop, where a "woman barber clips and combs and clips / a woman's hair." The woman is trembling and whimpering, while her "loving husband kneels, / consoling his frail wife in Polish, holding / her trembling hands in his big, clement hands." It is a tender and touching picture, rendered particularly unsettling by the sudden introduction of an image that hints at external violence in the last lines of the third stanza, as the couple leave the shop:

> where winter sunlight strikes the anvil street,
> and helicopter blades of light leap out
> from windshields in the supermarket lot.

This disconcerting effect is exacerbated in the final lines of the poem, when the second-person addressee of the poem himself leaves the shop, after having sat for the barber.

> Her touch, all business, has a healing power
> but not enough, or not enough for you.
> And when you pay and leave and feel the cold,
> the dicing blades of light will scatter you.

This conveys in highly effective manner the sense of disquietude caused by the sight of other people's grief.

Nothing could be more different than the poem that immediately succeeds this one. This is the first poem that clearly responds to the desire, expressed in the first poem of the book, for a *kéfi*-inspired "song" to carry us along. Its title is jauntily alliterative, with an internal rhyme: "**Sarong Song**." It is clearly addressed to Mason's new Australian partner, soon to be his wife, and abounds in images that associate her with the idea of travel to another world, particularly travel across the sea. The blueness of her sarong and, in the last stanza, of her eyes is clearly connected with the ocean:

> The woman in the blue sarong
> bade me believe in ships.
> *Come sail with me, the journey's long,*
> sang her alluring lips

The poem is joyous, mysterious, and (as the pun in the final line does more than hint) splendidly sexy:

> *Untie the sarong, my bonny boy,*
> *and bare me to the skies.*

The association of his beloved with water continues in the next poem, "**Necessity**," in which the poet, far from his lover, takes consolation in watching a creek, observing how it "falls as it must, / called by downhill, called by the waxing moon." This necessity of descent is intriguingly described as "the bed-ward conversation," suggesting that the stream's babble ("The water talks like an old woman known / for knowing names of every man she touched") is linked to sexual urges. By the end of the poem, the speaker merges his being with the water: "I think again of you / who love the water and are far away, / and I go falling where the water goes."

A similar desire is the subject of the next poem, "**The Tarmac**," though this is a much more anguished and intensely personal work ("Trained in deafness, you soon went blind"). The desire to escape "egocentric pain" finds relief in a sense of "letting go," described again as a yielding to the impulse of the waters of the world:

> You must go by the way of mountain tides,
> coral blizzards and the sunlit rain.

"**Let It Go**" is the title of a poem a couple of pages further on. This is a more discursive text, consisting of five nine-line stanzas, unrhyming except for the final couplet of each stanza, in which the poet addresses the Earth itself; as he says in stanza three, "Sometimes I hate you for coming between my love / and me," since his love is currently on the other side of the planet, "an ocean away." The poem began with his walking alone "on a trail of blooming dryad," as night comes on, with the sound of "the far-off traffic of a night-denying city." It concludes with a carefully constructed sentence in which he is now "walking down" the same path, drawn by the sound of

> the stream
> below me in the canyon, below the road,
> below the traffic of ambition and denial,
> the unclear water running to the sea,
> the stream, dear Earth, between my love and me.

Walking down the path is an act both of relinquishment—he declares that he is "shedding what I own"—and of reconciliation; he no longer hates the Earth for separating him from his love. Yielding to the motion of the stream, he recognizes that it is "running to the sea," and in the last line, the repetition of the words "the stream" suggests that the sea itself is a stream "between my love and me"—and hence it no longer separates him from his love but bears him toward her.

The eventual serenity of tone in this poem distinguishes it from the two shorter poems that preceded it, which are among the most intense and heartfelt in the book. **"Another Thing"** is the second sonnet in the volume, and it presents in highly concentrated, even cryptic, form a series of images connected with the notion of marine salvation—a notion that has begun to characterize the book. Like the poem that precedes it, "The Tarmac," it is written in the second person. Whereas "The Tarmac" seems dominated by a tone of fierce self-accusation, "Another Thing" is more reflective and proceeds by self-questioning, before finding a resolutory imperative in the final three lines.

A series of memorably enigmatic images pack the opening quatrain of the sonnet, all linked, as clearly stated in line two, to the notion of absence:

> Like fossil shells embedded in a stone,
> you are an absence, rimmed calligraphy,
> a mouthing out of silence, a way to see
> beyond the bedroom where you lie alone.

Fossil shells, of course, are a testimony to what is no longer present, and so the message they convey, in delicate but constricted form ("rimmed calligraphy"), is one of vacancy; line three suggests a futile attempt at communication, defeated by the sense of solitude, abandoned as he seems to be by his lover. This leads to the urgent proposals of the second quatrain, which take up the notion of loneliness in images that carry us into a more immense void: that of the skies and the oceans. The "vast, antipodal cloud" (with possibly a deliberate echo of Wordsworth's "lonely as a cloud") suggests that the trigger for this poem was the poet's solitude while his partner was in Australia; the solution is to embrace this state and to seek a salvific fusion with the great forces of nature:

> So why not be the vast, antipodal cloud
> you soloed under, riven by cold gales?
> And why not be the song of diving whales,
> why not the plosive surf below the road?

There is wonderful sonic play in these lines; the repeated 'o's seem to gesture toward the imagery of the opening lines, while they also convey the sense of a magnificent marine (and indeed *sub*marine) music.

The sestet continues with the imagery of marine travel; the first three lines gesture to "[t]he others," who are presented as single-minded and sure of their bearings:

> The others are one thing. They know they are.
> One compass needle. They have found their way
> and navigate by perfect cynosure.

"Cynosure" is another name for the North Star, but by its connotations it also suggests the self-confidence of those who are accustomed to being the center of attention. The last three lines continue with the second-person address, but whereas in the octave advice had been put in the form of propositional questions, now the speaker uses a plain imperative. The advice is radical, seeming to suggest that the way to salvation is through deliberate destruction of the old self.

> Go wreck yourself once more against the day
> and wash up like a bottle on the shore,
> lucidity and salt in all you say.

The language is still that of the sea, with the final image offering us an age-old image of hope amidst calamity—the message of the shipwrecked mariner, entrusted to a bottle. "[L]ucidity and salt" are the qualities conferred by this desperate/hopeful sea journey—and, of course, they are highly desirable qualities in poetry. Salt will recur as an image associated with love in a number of other poems—including the title poem of the volume.

The poem that immediately follows the sonnet, "**Prayer to the Air**," is much more desperate and urgent in tone. As the title indicates, it is in the form of a prayer. Nearly all of the lines are anaphoric, while each stanza ends in the same pleading refrain: "Teach me. Teach me." After the intensity of these desperate pleas, the subsequent poem, with its calming title, "**Let It Go**," comes as something of a relief.

As already indicated, it concludes with the idea of the sea as a means of reconciliation rather than of separation.

After a short poem titled "**4 July 11**," in which the poet feels strangely alienated from the national celebrations, the setting changes to Great Britain, in a number of poems recalling a visit there, with Chrissy, in the summer of 2011. The first two poems of this group are dedicated to his mother, who died that July, while he and Chrissy were traveling in Wales. One of them has the self-explanatory title, "**When I Didn't Get the News**" and the other "**14 July 11**," the date of his mother's death. The first poem, in free verse, begins with a description of the Welsh countryside, evoking the calm ordinariness of the day, which "marshaled me to peace." Eventually, as he puts it, his computer got the news: "the simple fact that you were dead / and that I'd missed the whole final drama / while in my life." The last four words emphasize the contrast between his and Chrissy's intensity of living and his mother's "final drama," a contrast that is enlarged upon in a meditative passage after an ellipsis. The poem ends with a moving evocation of his mother's achievement of serenity in her final years, throwing in some homely adages, presumably evocative of his mother: "No sense in grinding it to sausage, / no sense in cooking it to the perfect / killing meal."

The other short elegy for his mother begins with the simple question, *"Where does a life go?"* Simple, but unanswerable for someone who "can't go / where the holy rollers go." He takes as his symbol for life's fugacity "the clouds [...] above the hills at Brecon," trees, blown roses and his love "all cloud, / all rain, I reckon." There is perhaps a hint that the final image brings with it not just the notion of dispersion but also that of eventual fruitfulness.

The next poems are love poems, still in a British setting, and with a constant presence of water. In "**Salmon Leap**," the elegiac tone remains, with "the sound of water" providing the only reliable constant in a world marked by loss; the final stanza suggests that even as our ashes have been "washed away by rain," our voices will have been merged into this music so that "we will speak aloud / the language of a watery refrain, / clear as any cloud."

In "**Night and My Love**," the "voice / of water" is described as "pending evermore," while the night is evoked as a "current" that might bring some solace to his beloved, unable to sleep because of "pain I can do nothing to assuage." "**All Change**," written in short couplets, brings the imagery of the salmon-bearing river to London, with a series of flickering images providing memorable glimpses of his lover in urban settings. The "*All change, all change*" cry of the underground trains seems particularly well suited to his lover, seen as a "river maiden" who "plunges hands / in the lukewarm Thames, // the brown eddy and flow, / and calls it blessed." The odd syntactical shift in the next three lines, "You've seen her swim / in total delight // and weather change," seems particularly suited to his lover's protean character. The poem concludes with the declaration, "Water's her nature // and water's life / there for the drinking." The last London poem is "**The Quire**," in which his lover is seen paying tearful homage to the tomb of Donne, "tears erupt[ing] / from lines a lifetime gone."

It is followed by one of the shortest poems in the book, just four lines long, "**Lop-Sided Prayer**." It could be said to serve as a more compact and far more powerful restatement of the sentiments in the rather overwrought "Prayer to the Air." It consists of just two rhyming couplets, both subtle reflections on influence, and on cause and effect, with a final plea for authenticity of feeling:

> Bluejoint, fescue, foxglove, bee-sipped daisies
> Sign to the breeze what its direction is.
>
> Night bleeds into everything you see.
> Oh please be you. And please let me be me.

The remaining poems in the second section seem to return to an American setting, most of them being set on the coast of Oregon; this was where Chrissy chose to settle, having found the climate of Colorado too dry for her, so that Mason divided his time between Colorado and the coast. Such poems as "The Oregon Way," "At the Sylvia Beach Hotel," "Seaside Distances," "A Tree Light House," and "Blue of the Bay" clearly draw on or describe this new scenery. Many of these are love poems in which the landscape sometimes plays an unexpected role. An example is "**The Oregon Way**," where the damp climate of the region is evoked in almost Petrarchan fashion: "Wring out the clouds, my lady. / Tumble them into your arms." In

"**The Seaside Distances**," a lover's quarrel takes place in the "inhuman space" of the beach, where the "crabbing gulls" seem to be engaged in a similar quarrel, and "each curled pursuing wave" recalls to the speaker the something in him "that died when [she] walked out / to nurse a hurt."

"**River Days**" returns us to Colorado, presumably during a visit of Chrissy's. It is a poem of gratitude, both for the beauty of nature, showing its "abundance even in a desert," and for the gift of his lover's presence, which is perhaps what lies behind the speaker's heightened awareness of the animation of the landscape: "that gneiss and pegamite should color cliffs / cut by the green river laughing below // is cause enough for praise." The poem concludes with the stanza we quoted in our discussion of *The Country I Remember*, suggesting that it could serve as a coda to the interwoven stories of that narrative; perhaps, more pertinently, it could be seen as pointing to a central leitmotif of all Mason's poetry:

> Like others of our kind we move toward water,
> not only to slake our thirst
> but also because it binds us,
> our tides and metamorphoses, our bed
> of scars, our love, our passing.

The section concludes with three short love poems, of varying degrees of mystery. The first is perhaps the strangest. The title, "**She Is**," leads immediately into the striking but rather unsettling line "a small wolf eating a caul." The poem is written in irregular two-line stanzas, with the exception of this opening line and the equally disturbing line eight, "after the slaughter." The stanzas, each of which presents a single resonant image, rhyme between themselves, thus attenuating the sense of fragmentation. Some of the images suggest pain and loss: "a girl holding the leg / of a broken doll" and "a hurt tune / lying still in a dark room," but there are also hints of salvific beauty—"warm gold in the water / but a cool dawn"—and of acute sensitivity—"a sine curve / in a line of thought // all nerve / uncaught." "**Chrismata,**" which follows this cryptic poem, reflects on the unknowable mysterious nature of his lover, who was "not formed by origins." The last three lines evoke a sense of ritual rebirth through "fresh anointings," recalling the image of salt, so important in this volume: "salt, baptismal rain."

The last poem in the section, "**The Soul Fox,**" is one of his most moving. It is dedicated to Chrissy and dated "28 October 2011." It marks the return of the image of the fox in this book, already seen in "New World" and soon to reappear in "Andritsena Revisited"; in all three cases, the sight of this elusive animal is celebrated as something marvelous, almost miraculous. "Soul Fox," even in its title, echoes Ted Hughes's famous poem "The Thought Fox," in which the fox clearly symbolized poetic inspiration. In Hughes's poem, the fox is not seen but imagined, being brought to life piece by piece until the final stanza, when "with a sudden sharp hot stink of fox / It enters the dark hole of the head. / The window is starless still: the clock ticks, / The page is printed."

Mason has declared that his poem was written as a reaction to the death of the American psychologist James Hillman, the founder of archetypal psychology, whose works are said to have restored the word "soul" to its psychological sense. Chrissy is an intense admirer of Hillman's works, and the poem is a tribute both to her and to her mentor. But the poem begins with the sight of a real fox, and it is presented as an event they have both participated in: "My love, the fox is in the yard." The description of what they have seen—"we who saw / his way of finding out, his night / of seeking"—clearly applies also to the works of Hillman, which is another shared experience; they "are the better for it." The simple imperative word that follows—"Write"—seems to be addressed to them both. Although the image of the melting snow indicates the ephemeral nature of literary efforts, the concluding rhyming couplet, stated in cohortative mood, expresses a joy in the activity itself: "Let the white page bear the mark, / then melt with joy upon the dark." The last word of the poem is "dark," but it nonetheless strikes the reader as essentially a celebratory poem, and what it celebrates is the shared nature of their literary life.

The final section of the book contains an interesting miscellany of poems, testifying to Mason's versatility. Some of them look back to episodes and memories from his past, although the poems in the final group are clearly set on the Oregon coast again. It is perhaps worth beginning our discussion of the section by looking at its longest poem, "**Mrs. Mason and the Poets**," which is something of an anomaly, even though from its title it would appear to belong to the category of family poems.

This poem, which was included in *Best American Poetry 2012*, turns out to be a monologue by a friend of the poet Shelley. "Mrs. Mason" was in fact an Irish aristocrat, living in Pisa with an Englishman, Mr. Tighe; they had adopted a common surname with the aim of "domesticating the arrangement." The poem succeeds in throwing a new light on Shelley and his circle by means of the curious contrast between the placid, civilized tones of the speaker and the extravagant behavior of the poetic world with which she has come into contact. One has the impression of a delicate and restrained sense of irony governing her words, as when she describes Shelley's "brilliant wife" as "palely loitering." Although it is difficult to believe that a lady of this sort would be consciously alluding to Keats (or, indeed, to Marvell, just a few lines later: "Shelley of the godless vegetable love"), the literary references contribute to our sense of her as an ironic observer of the tormented excesses of these romantic souls. It is as if a character from a Jane Austen novel had strayed into the Byron-Shelley world:

> Genius, yes, but often idiotic.
> It took too many deaths, too many drownings,
> fevers, accusations, to make him see
> the ordinary life was not all bad.

She herself has her vision of Shelley after death, however; Mason transcribes almost word-for-word the lines of dialogue from her dream as reported in Edmund Blunden's biography of the poet, making only the slightest adjustment for the sake of meter. Her sad realization that Shelley had drowned takes on extra poignancy, from the play of moods and registers. "To see such brightness fallen broke my heart," she declares, and one senses the fascination the young poet had exerted on her. The poem ends in melancholy mood, as she imagines the dialogue with her "husband" when he returns from his stroll. Affected by the romantic mood of her memories, she confers a touch of ethereal (and slightly comic) beauty even on Mr. Tighe: "And I shall notice how a slight peach flush / illuminates his whiskers as the sun / rounds the palms and enters at our windows." The poem ends with her accepting her husband's consolation: "And I? What shall I say to this kind man / but *Yes, my darling, time to pour the wine.*" And we return to a world of rules, where each daily ritual has its set time and place. The poem is wonderfully poised between humor and touching sadness; it is different from anything he has written before.

Many of the other poems, as already indicated, draw on memories from his past. The first poem, "**Amaknak**," recalls his days on the crab boat in Alaska. It is a return to the topic he had explored in "Mise en Scène" in *Arrivals*, although this time the emphasis on violence is even more marked, with the word "Death" recurring in the tightly rhyming six-line stanzas like a grim knell.

This poem presents an imaginative revisiting of a place of his youth, whereas a number of other poems, such as **"Andritsena Revisited"** and "The Bay of Writing," derive from physical returns to his former haunts. The first poem, consisting of two unrhyming sonnets (and containing the third fox in the volume), depicts a journey back to a place which had been the setting for the touching narrative "The Nightingales of Andritsena" in his first full-length collection. The sonnets are remarkable for their long sentences, which in their syntactical intricacy capture the working of the speaker's mind, as he compares past and present; the contrast between the two and their simultaneous interweaving find a curious counterpoint in the way the speaker moves between the "privately fruitful" world of the mysterious temple, deep in the "secret woods," and the village, with its cooking smells and barking dogs.

"The Bay of Writing" had concluded his memoir, *News from the Village*, and it reflects on the name of the bay of his former home, *Kalamitsi*, literally bay of reeds. Since the word *kalamus* means both reed and a pen, Mason can play upon the notion that the place is also a Bay of Writing. He uses an epigraph from Seferis (*"And I with only a reed in my hands"*) and evokes Sappho and Archilochos, thus allying himself with the long tradition of Greek poetry. The epigraph suggests that, rather than being written *in loco*, Mason is simply musing on a reed, "dried and cut," which allows him to return "in retrospect" to the bay. He recalls "the lazy hours / watching the ant roads through the summer straw," which taught him "the frantic diligence of mind." The poem thus manages to evoke simultaneously a sense of physical relaxation ("the lazy hours") and one of intense mental activity. The final lines, "*Kalamitsi, Kalamitsi,* bay of reeds, / music of everything I have not written," seem to allude to the image of the "pan-pipe / on an idle day" that opened the poem. Mason has stated that the poem was originally dedicated to Patrick Leigh Fermor, the other writer who lived on the bay (who was still alive when the poem was written). There is perhaps here an allusion to the sad fact that his great trilogy of travel books was destined never to be finished.

The workings of memory are also hinted at in other poems, such as "**Marco Polo in the Old Hotel,**" in which a hotel guest sipping wine ("another glass of sunlight") after dinner lets the echoing voices of children, as they play their game of tag in the pool, take him back "through the evenings, years / and decades of late summer weather." The final stanza uses imagery suggested by the name of the explorer ("a flag / is flapping, thin as Chinese silk / the camels caravanned through deserts") to evoke the notion of the limitless travel of the recalling mind:

> You breathe the last mouthful of wine
> and seem to float into the air
> as they call to eternity,
> the unenclosing everywhere:

Marco ...

... Polo

Marco ...

... Polo

There is something Larkinesque in these final lines, which remind one of the haunting images that close such poems as "Here" and "High Windows."

The poem **"Fog Horns"** also plays with echoing sounds, using synesthesia ("and purple fog horns / blossomed over tides") to evoke a world of damp indistinctness where sound and sight blur into one another, and time becomes strangely meaningless. The poem, written in syllabics, has a haunting sonority, with rhyming tercets (each line just five syllables) and frequent "o" sounds, which suggest the melancholy and mysterious music of the horns. Mason has indicated that it is actually an ekphrastic poem, being inspired by a 1929 painting by Arthur Dove with almost exactly the same title ("Foghorns"), which is on exhibit at the Colorado Springs Fine Arts Center. The lack of any clear reference to the painting can be considered as in keeping with the poem's deliberate air of mystery.

The last three poems of the volume return us to the western coast of North America, where Mason's wife had moved into in a house by the ocean, which provides the setting for the poem titled **"Tree Light House."** All three words, deliberately not connected by hyphens, can be seen as crucial to the poem, which suggests that the house, in its airy openness and its propinquity to the trees and the ocean, has healing qualities both for his wife, who is "feverish" at the beginning of the poem, and for the poet himself. As in a long tradition of environmentally aware literature, the poem celebrates the virtue of "relinquishment," while the poet, in his caring activities, learns to feel "again / the original touch / of the world." As in the earlier poems about the poet's partner, she is closely associated with imagery of the sea; even the "rasp of [her] cough" is compared to "surf over gravel." The speaker's tender ministrations are associated with the rocking activity of the ocean, and in the final lines he describes them both as living "in the breathing clock of the sea, / the whalesong of memory." The final words, "Lighten me," suggest a desire both for illumination and for the weightless sensation of a body that has surrendered to the waves.

"**The Blue of the Bay**," the penultimate poem in the book, is written in rhyming tercets with a prevalently anapestic rhythm, which gives it something of the lilting music of a sea shanty—a music that is rather at odds with the brutality of some of the imagery:

> The bird on its back lying dead on the shore,
> its breast torn open, its hollow core—
> what more can be learned of the bird on the shore?

The last three stanzas revert to the imagery of the tidal tug, which had played so strong a role in earlier poems in the book:

The moon held fast in the undertow.
I felt it pulling me, strong and slow,
the long withdrawing undertow

The final poem, "**Sea Salt**," which gives its title to the book, is curiously impersonal, with only one punning use of the first person in the final stanza: "The days are made of hours, / hours of instances, / and none of them are ours." Otherwise, the four six-line stanzas seem to depict the marine setting with peculiar, almost inhuman detachment. The day's phenomena are all described as if they are separate and wholly random events; even a kite that "nods to its string" seems to be connected to no human agency. We are told that "A cloud is happening," and when it is "joined by another crowd," they are "a crowd that moves." The poem moves from dazzling light in the opening lines to darkening light in the final lines. There is a curious echo of the final stanza of "Fog Horns," in which "Nothing was ever / done. Then it was done." In this poem, instead, we are told: "There's nothing to be done." But the apparent bleakness of this statement is offset by the repeated assurance: "This too shall come to pass," which actually concludes the poem. The overall tone seems to be one of calm acceptance—an embracing of the paradoxical condition of the sea, which "stands still and moves."

It suggests that the poet has indeed followed the instruction given in the sonnet, "Another Thing," and wrecked himself "against the day" to "wash up like a bottle against the shore." Coming as it does at the end of a volume of poems that have drawn on and depicted a wide variety of emotional states, from despair to hope, from guilt to celebration, from self-loathing to ardent love, this poem, with its mysteriously dispassionate composure ("lucidity and salt in all you say," in the words of the sonnet), provides a sense of true conclusion, while at the same time gesturing to possibilities of further emotional development.

CHAPTER 8

Davey McGravy

One year after the publication of *Sea Salt*, Paul Dry Books brought out David Mason's first (and so far only) book for children, *Davey McGravy*. The rhyming title gives a strong hint not only of the form of the narrative (mainly in rhyming quatrains) but also of its underlying theme. As Mason put it an interview, from the moment the child protagonist is given a rhyming name by his father, "it works a kind of magic. Davey begins to see rhymes—correspondences—everywhere in nature, even in those parts of nature we find in the shopping mall and in school."

The novel begins with what seems like a dedication—"To Love"—but turns out to be an address to the reader. Or, perhaps more aptly, to the listener, since the book is clearly designed also to be read aloud. As Mason has put it, "I decided the storyteller was a child reading to a parent or a parent reading to a child." In either case, the emphasis is on a bond of love, which we feel extended to ourselves as well. The risk of over-sentimentality is avoided by the wry conclusion in the final quatrain:

… as you too were a babe,

with parents and the whole canoe,
the whole catastrophe
we call a family—
the human zoo.

Although "canoe" may seem at first a little odd, it
works well with the setting that has been depicted in the
opening stanzas of this address, which clearly draws on the
Washington State of Mason's own childhood:

You need only know he was born
in the land of rain
and the tallest of tall tees—

great shaggy cedars like the boots
of giants covered in green

What is a simple but effective simile in these opening
stanzas becomes an imaginative truth for the child Davey,
who "thought he saw the giants / outside in the woods,
looking, / looking for their lost boots." Meeting the skep-
ticism of his brothers, both Big and Little, he learns to
keep "to himself / the secret of what he saw." The same
will apply to his perception that "Sometimes wind was a
stream / far, far up in the trees / and birds went swimming
through the air." Big Brother instructs him, "You can't
say crazy things like that." But as Charles Martin put it in
his blurb for the book, the story will show how "through
heartbreaking loss" Davey discovers—and learns to trea-
sure—"the transformative powers of the imagination."

The loss comes with the mysterious disappearance of the children's mother, who, we are told, "fell into a fog and left." The children's grief and bewilderment are touchingly evoked, and we hear how Davey, hugging his father by his leg, gets his new name:

> "Davey McGravy," he said again,
> "How's that for a brand new name?
> Davey McGravy. Not so bad.
> I like a name that rhymes."

The magic of rhyme, it becomes clear as the story proceeds, lies at the heart of the poem. It's a magic that confers a new kind of relationship with the natural world that surrounds the child. Davey lies awake that night "singing his secret song":

> *Davey McGravy, Davey McGravy,*
> *a name to conjure with.*
> *I like a name that rhymes,*
> *and waves like waves on the lake.*
>
> *It sounds like rain on a window.*
> *It sounds like wind in the trees.*
> *It sounds like a fern in the forest*
> *waving in the breeze.*

The name both rhymes and "waves"—and the ambiguity of the second verb allows us to imagine the child's name both undulating in harmony with the lake and signaling to the world. And indeed, as the child goes out into the woods, he perceives that "the trees waved." This beckoning draws him on, and he sets forth to explore "all the world abounding." The child's sensuous discovery of the rich, waterlogged surroundings of his house is described effectively; realistic details, like the "touch of the web" that stayed with him, "light as a breath," and the "squishy sound" of a "giant cedar log, / wet and rotting on the ground," go hand in hand with the child's imaginative vision of the mist as "wet smoke from an ancient fire / back in the giants' day."

In this first woodland escape, Davey meets a talking peacock, who announces that his "rainbow eyes," just like Davey's name, "are a kind of rhyme." Rhyme, it seems, is a key to understanding the world and can also offer solace for its sorrows:

> "And rain is a kind of rhyme,
> and so are two halves of a leaf.
> And maybe you walked out in the woods
> to rhyme away your grief."

The narrative proceeds with a series of magical encounters with talking birds and animals, each one acting like a narrative rhyme with the preceding ones. The same is true of the series of dream flights that Davey experiences; through the power of rhyme, he learns to rely on the imaginative truth of these adventures, mocked though they are by his skeptical brothers and schoolmates:

> The things that happened in his mind
> and things that happened in the day

happened together like a rhyme.
And he could fly!

Mason avoids monotony by varying the settings for
these adventures. The first flight is by day, with the child
tumbling "around like a wind-blown cloud / without a
single care." The second takes place at night, with Davey
encountering talkative bats, who tell him that "blindness
doesn't matter [...] when you're Davey McGravy. // You
can dream yourself over the water / and over the lights of
the town ..." The final dream flight is experienced when
Davey runs away from school to the docks; feeling rejected by his schoolmates, this time he finds himself flying to
the town garbage mound with the seagulls.

In the shopping mall, after a mysterious and agoniz-
ing glimpse of his mother on an escalator, he encounters
a talking cockatoo. It is probably no accident that the
cockatoo is Australian and is nostalgic for its "far country," much like Mason's wife at the time of writing.[1] Mason
clearly enjoys adding a touch of Australian vigor and humor to the narrative at this point, as the bird encourages
Davey to join in its crazy dance. The quatrain is extended
to a supple ten-line stanza, full of jingling internal rhymes:

"I'm free," said the hopping cockatoo,
"as long as I can dance.

1. According to Mason, the poem was inspired by Chrissy, who, on learning
that David's father had nicknamed him Davey McGravy, "saw immediately that
[the name] was already a book" and that he was "fated to write it."

Like you I fly all night in my dreams.
I whistle and shriek and laugh and scream
like a girl with ants in her pants!
These other birds think I'm absurd.
It doesn't matter what they say.
I'm like a kid with a rhyming name,
lost in the woods but all the same
I still know how to play!"

We also see Davey at school, where his imaginative fancies are mocked by other children. But while in class, he listens to a poem by Robert Louis Stevenson, which could well have provided the inspiration for the whole book:

"All by myself I have to go,
With none to tell what to do—
All alone beside the streams
And up the mountain-side of dreams."

The final chapter, as if picking up on the suggestions of Stevenson's lines, returns us to the forest setting of the early chapters. This time, the imagery of dampness and mystery is taken to another level. The chapter begins by evoking, once again with effective internal rhymes, the sounds of the waves on the shore that "slap and hush and suck and slap, / then lap and slap some more." This is an effective introduction to the rhythm and music of this chapter, in which Davey will have his most moving encounter with a creature of the woods, in a beautifully depicted autumnal fog.

This time, the creatures of the woods are far less garrulous. The crow who summons him to this encounter limits himself to a few words, mainly a reminder of those earlier statements on the significance of his rhyming name:

> "Remember who you are," said the crow,
> "Remember the things that rhyme,
> like two sides of a leaf, like rain.
> Remember the time."

The encounter is with a mountain lioness, and it takes place entirely in silence, with the child sure that he is going to die. Instead, at the crow's beckoning, he climbs onto the lioness's back. We are given the realistic detail, "He felt the muscles of her back, / smelled forest fog from her fur," and he is then carried back to his house:

> The boy, the crow and the lioness
> moved through woods still dripping,
> ferns and nettles and bright salal,
> the long tail swishing.

Davey is brought back to his father, whose leg he once again hugs, and the narrator resumes his address to the reader:

> And Love, that's where we'll leave them,
> in the green house by the lake,
> and the land of rain and tall, tall trees
> where birds go swimming in the breeze
> and fish fly in the waves [...]

This is no longer presented just as Davey's perception of his surroundings. His series of imaginative encounters with the wise and strange creatures of the world are recalled in the final stanzas, as well as the friends he has made at school. Perhaps wishing to connect with the world of twenty-first-century children, Mason gives he last line of the poem to Davey's friend Alice, who possesses a telephone.

The book, which is embellished with illustrations by Grant Silverstein, testifies to Mason's wish to explore new fields. While it clearly draws on his own experiences as an imaginative child who grew up in Washington State (the landscape is similar to that evoked in some of his earlier poems, such as "A Meaning Made of Trees"), the music of its verse, with its interweaving rhymes and its haunting refrains, is entirely fresh. Despite the melancholy theme, the narrative has a vigor and an essential inner joy that it might not be too presumptuous to attribute to the new prospects opened up to him by his marriage to Chrissy, a poet from Australia. "If you watch me dance / it'll teach you a thing or two about life / you can learn at a glance," says the cockatoo, to Davey.

This is not to suggest that crazy dance rhythms have become dominant features of his new poetry. Rather, I wish to point to a sense of a broadening of horizons—literal as well as metaphorical—that is clearly discernible in the number of new paths he has begun to explore, which range from prose fiction to opera libretti, in addition to poetry that celebrates the strange landscapes of his new home.

CHAPTER 9

Words for Music

David Mason's most important new venture over the past few years has been his entrance into the world of opera. After hearing one of his poems turned into an art song by the composer Lori Laitman, he collaborated with her on an operatic version of *The Scarlet Letter*. The libretto was published in 2012 by Red Hen Press with the title *The Scarlet Libretto*, and the opera was eventually premiered by Opera Colorado in 2016. He has also written a libretto for an oratorio, *Vedem*, based on the experiences of children at the concentration camp of Terezin, again with music by Lori Laitman. *Vedem* was first performed in Seattle in 2010. Laitman has also collaborated with him on an operatic version of *Ludlow*, which is still awaiting performance, although excerpts have been published by Enchanted Knickers Music.

With the composer Tom Cipullo he has written two short operas, one about the lives of Picasso and Gertrude Stein in Paris under the Nazis, titled *After Life* and another

about the final days of the Hungarian poet Miklós Radnóti titled *The Parting*; both premiered at Music of Remembrance, Seattle, in May 2015 and May 2019, respectively.
All but *Ludlow* are available on compact disc from the
Naxos label.

In the preface to **The Scarlet Libretto**, Mason explains
how the idea of the opera first arose and his method of
working. As one might expect, his principal model is
W. H. Auden. But he distances himself from some of
Auden's pronouncements on writing librettos—for example, the notion that words are the most expendable of the
three elements that the librettist has to furnish the composer with (the other two being plot and characters). Mason points out that "modern audiences do want to know
at least some of the words, which is why modern opera
companies often use surtitles." Furthermore, he states that
Lori Laitman is a composer "who loves and is constantly
inspired by words." His task, as he saw it, was "less to guide
her inspiration than to liberate it."

One of the most effective features of the libretto is the
role he creates for the chorus of townspeople. The words
of the chorus serve to establish the conservative ethos of
the town, which is what has condemned and isolated Hes-
ter. As Mason puts it, their verses delineate "the absolut-
ist stance that underlies religious fundamentalism." This
comes across in their grim declaration, repeated at the beginning and end of the opera:

One law for the sea we crossed.
One law for the forest dark.
One law for the savage heart
One law for the babe in arms.

As Mason says in the preface, his job as librettist "is not just to convey the idea, but also to provide a striking enough refrain: 'One law. One law. One law. One.'"

Of course, a good deal of the novel has to be stripped away to create an effective and performable libretto. Even so, it is striking how much Mason manages to communicate of the novel's power, without falling into simplification or sensationalism. A key concept, for which he finds poetic expression, is that "the story falls back into a pool of time, seen from a distance like some nagging seed at the source of ancestral American guilt." He thus creates a choral interlude for the passing of time:

Time is vaster than the earth.
Time is larger than our law.
Time before all human birth
and all we have no image for.

Toward the end of the preface, Mason states that "the historical sense of this libretto links it to other books of mine, including *The Country I Remember* and *Ludlow*. Readers are welcome to see it as part of an idiosyncratic vision of America in verse."

His second libretto deals again with a historical theme, the most tragic of the previous century. ***Vedem*** was commissioned by Seattle's Music of Remembrance, a chamber music organization devoted to remembering Holocaust musicians and their art. The oratorio commemorates a group of teenage boys from Prague who, in the concentration camp of Terezin, put together a magazine called *VEDEM* (Czech for "In the lead"); the manuscript was buried and later dug up by one of the surviving boys, Sidney Taussig, who was actually present at the performance of the oratorio. Lori Laitman set some of the boys' poems to music, and subsequently Mason wrote lyrics linking the poems; the boys describe their lives in the camp, their hopes and fears, and their determination to "make beauty to delay our death." The oratorio begins with a man pleading to be heard:

> Hear my story as it comes to me,
> for I am vanished from the world you love,
> and I am nothing without memory.

This plea is taken up by the chorus of children, restated now in the plural, with the constant refrain, "Hear our story now. / Hear our story now, oh hear." The oratorio mingles memories of ghetto life with accounts of how the children organized themselves around their magazine: "we lived for what we wrote and painted, / as if imagination were a jewel." The oratorio ends with a litany of names: "The names go on and on. [...] All to oblivion." The last words repeat the plea to be remembered: "Remember us. Remember us. / We were no different than you." Perhaps the theme of memory, so central to Mason's poetry, has never been given more poignant expression.

After Life was also commissioned by Music of Remembrance. It presents two iconic figures of modernism, Pablo Picasso and Gertrude Stein, confronting each other in a realm of the afterlife, and bickering on their experiences in France under the Nazis. The situation serves Mason, as he has stated in a preface he prepared for the libretto, to create "a story about artists in relation to history—the darkest history imaginable." He clearly has some fun in creating a voice for Stein that reminds us of her verbal style:

> Baby Precious? Is it you?
> Baby, long, how long, is it who?
>
> Sound of a sigh ... I.
> I was the cover of TIME. I.
> Everyone loved me. I
> want you, Mr. Cuddle-Wuddle.
> Oh what a muddle!
> How is it I is it who?

Picasso is rather less caricatured, but Mason conveys something of his massive ego in his rage at Stein's insistence that it was she who had created him. Picasso indicates another meaning of the title: "The afterlife, you say. I was always / after life, after love. I bathed in the sun! [...] Life! After life. Art is for life!"

The comedy turns sour, however, with the introduction of a third character, a young woman who was taken from an orphanage to a concentration camp. She is the incarnation of anonymity, a figure whom nobody knew in life and whose death is unrecorded and unremembered. The encounter with this figure seems at last to strip the two artists of their Cleopatra-like "immortal longings." As Mason says in his preface, "It is she who must make them understand what death is, and that they have not finished dying as human beings." In an ironic twist, the young woman tells Stein, "The cover of time is gone," stripping the word of its capital letter. She has the final words, which consist of one final memory: "I remember—what do I remember? / That April was cold. / Cold, so cold. / That April was cold."

The Parting again deals with the theme of the Holocaust, this time focusing on the figure of the poet Miklós Radnóti on his last night in his Budapest apartment before being drafted into forced labor; he would eventually be shot during a forced march. The libretto incorporates numerous poems from the notebook that was found on his body when it was recovered from the mass grave into which it had been thrown after his execution. The three characters in the opera are the poet, his wife Fanni Gyarmati, and Death. This last figure is a mezzo-soprano, and she is presented as curiously compassionate. Both Fanni and Miklós separately ask her what the point of living is; to Fanni she responds, "To learn about love," and to Miklós, "To learn what love is. To love. / To make beautiful things. To die."

It is Death who tells us how Miklós's life will end, even down to the detail of Fanni's trying to recognize his bones by the red jumper she had earlier darned for him. The opera concludes with jointly sung lyrics, which, as Death has told us, are "the songs from a dead man's coat." The notebook containing the songs plays a prominent role in the opera; a key stage direction reads, "FIF picks up the notebook as if seeing it for the first time, breathes deeply and lovingly hands it to MIK. He grips the notebook, also breathes deeply, then puts it in the pocket of his overcoat, turning back to FIF."

Cipullo's music is rich and moving, beautifully rendering the tenderness between the couple and the agony of their parting, which they are fully aware is to be a final one. Nonetheless, the very last words of the opera are "I'm alive. / I'm alive." Tragic though the opera is, it is actually a hymn to life—and to art that has the power to celebrate living.

CHAPTER 10

The Sound

The Sound, published in 2018, was a milestone in a poet's career—a volume of new and selected poems. Following a well-established tradition, the book opens with the new poems, and the subsequent selections from the earlier volumes are in reverse chronological order, providing the effect, as Mason puts it in the title of his author's note, of a kind of "Walking Backwards." He included the narrative "The Country I Remember" but chose not to excerpt his verse novels, plays, and libretti. *Sea Salt* is excerpted generously, but the selections grow sparser and sparser as the book travels back in time, with his first volume, *The Buried Houses*, providing just six poems (although three of these are substantial narratives).

The author's note explains the title:

The Sound is a location, my place of origin and womb of words, but is also an aspiration and aural guide. "The sound is the gold in the ore," Frost wrote. One hears something and wants to make a corresponding sound. I have been hard of hearing all my life, catching vowels more than consonants, so the sound I follow is watery. I hope you can hear it too.

This note provides a helpful approach to the book, and particularly to the new poems. As we have already seen, many of his poems deal with memories of growing up on the island-strewn, water-indented coast of Washington State; in *Arrivals*, one poem is titled "Desolation Sound," while another, "Swimmers on the Shore," describes how "the salt breeze blows across the Sound." This was indeed his "place of origin and womb of words," and several of the new poems in *The Sound* return to the landscape of the Pacific Northwest (a vast area for Mason, stretching from Oregon to Alaska)—as well as to other places from his past, which we are made to both see and hear. Mason's mother worked with Native American children, and his father was a reservation psychiatrist for the Makah, a whaling tribe on the Olympic peninsula, and so he grew up immersed in the mythology of the place. His parents' memories will be central to a number of poems in the opening section.

The section of new poems begins with a striking un-rhyming sonnet, "**Descend**," which uses the metaphor of a marine submersion to suggest the idea of a rebirth and new beginning; the sonnet actually ends with the one-word imperative: "Begin." Coming as it does at the very outset of the volume, it perhaps reminds us of another meaning of the word "sound": to measure the depth of a mass of water. The sonnet instructs the reader (and listener) on how to "be reborn / to the changing light." It involves an escape from the chattering of those who "withered into hate" by a descent "among the voiceless where you have a voice, / barely a whisper, unheard by most, a wave / among the numberless waves ..." This ritualistic immersion prepares us for much of the watery imagery (and music) that will wash through the subsequent poems.

The next two poems include the figure of the poet's female companion. The first one, "**The World of Hurt**," in five unrhyming tercets, focuses on a moment in which the speaker is able to offer a single instance of hopeful deliverance from suffering—a bird that managed to save itself from crashing into a window. This offers a momentary respite from "the world of hurt" of the title. The second tercet succeeds in concentrating all this pain into two telling images, "expedient bombing / and frontiers brimming with refugees," pictures that the companion turns from "to face me, the hurt / taking hold in her eyes." It is at this point that the speaker sees the bird saving itself, describing how it "banked / before impact, and left like a song / and was gone to die some other way." Despite the wry realism of this last clause, the speaker, by recounting what he has seen, is able to change the look in his companion's eyes. The final line of the poem—"The bird that flew off into the world"—provides an uplifting note of salvific liberation, recalling perhaps a line from Richard Wilbur's poem "The Writer," about a bird in a bedroom that finally found the window and flew out, "clearing the sill of the world." Of course, even as we savor this sense of liberation, we cannot forget that "the world" the bird has flown off into is still "the world of hurt" of the title.

The second poem, in envelope-rhyming quatrains, is subtly erotic, as evidenced from its very title, **"Woman Dressing by a Window."** Ostensibly, it seems to lament the fact that words are inadequate to express the "fire between touch / and touch," while the graceful play of rhymes and alliteration serves to counter this notion, suggesting in the lithe enjambed movement of the lines the sensuous and lively movements of the woman, and the responses they provoke.

The next two poems return us to places from Mason's earlier working days. The fourth one, written in seven irregular rhyming tercets (with the penultimate one for some reason reduced to a couplet), serves as the title poem of the whole book, **"The Sound."** The landscape and imagery recall those of such poems as "Mise en Scène" and "Amaknak," which described his experiences on a crab boat in Alaska. In this poem, however, the landscape seems to be revisited in a dream, with the speaker responding to the commands of the "drunken skipper" with an improbable declaration of sturdy independence: "I said I work alone like all my kind." Despite the realistic technical details of the various tasks referred to ("the net drum, // the power block for brailing the wet line …"), the marine imagery seems to be employed toward the same metaphorical ends as in the first poem in the volume. The final tercet offers an intriguing image of pioneering audacity:

I headed for the point beyond the point
and stripped and greased myself with oolichan
and swam the echoes to oblivion.

Oolichan (or eulachon) is a small species of smelt so high in oil content that, when dried, it can be used as a candle. It was of great importance to Native Americans, who would use its oil to reanimate food that they had dried for the winter; Makah whalers would grease themselves with the oil, dive into the freezing sea waters, and sew up a harpooned whale's mouth so it would not fill with water and sink. Interestingly, it is also known as the "Savior fish," a name that seems appropriate to this poem.

The last line is curiously ambiguous, one possible interpretation being that the speaker in his swimming journey followed the echoes to final oblivion, while another reading, perhaps rather less bleak, could be that the speaker, by his swimming, succeeded in canceling the echoes. In either case, the poem testifies to the enduring hold that his Alaskan experiences, together with folklore learned from his parents' working lives, still have on the poet's mind.

The subsequent poem, **"Combine,"** is set on land, with the poet returning to memories of a summer job in the fields. The sound remains a clear presence, however, being mentioned in line ten, while "the smell of marsh salt" mingles with that of "chaff and rotting vines." The poem is intensely realistic in its physical description, with no idealization of the experience; he recalls such details as "a field mouse squirming / on the fork boy's tines" and focuses closely on the "work-swollen knuckles" of the mechanic's hands, with "one finger nipped off / at the top joint." But he notes that "The work was slow enough / for thought, still more for books / read in all weathers / when the bosses left," and the final lines evoke the two forms of learning that the boy is experiencing. This is a concern that Mason shares with Frost, who, in such poems as "Death of the Hired Man," "The Ax-Helve," and "From Plane to Plane," reflects upon and compares two kinds of knowledge, that of physical labor and that of intellectual study.

The Alaskan experience returns in the next poem, "**The Gifts of Time**," in blank-verse stanzas. But the poem begins in the house "high up in the trees," which we have already encountered in the poem "Tree Light House" (*Sea Salt*). It opens with a moment of blessed stasis, indicated by a calm infinitive: "To stand in the kitchen high up in trees / watching a sapling sway ..." We are told that this moment of meditation, "a mug of coffee in the hand," after decades of "necessary task[s]" is "all of time." The first stanza concludes with the simple sentence, "It's time to breathe."

The second stanza moves us out to sea (the closeness of which had already been hinted at in the first stanza by the metaphor of the "undersea" that stirred the "canopy of leaves and needles"), to a ship where "a young man standing on the bridge" has time "to wonder if that distant speck is bird / or continent." For those who know Mason's work, it is natural to wonder whether this young man, whom we next see with stethoscope listening to "the heartbeat of an ailing girl," is the poet's father, who became a doctor after his wartime service in the navy. In the third stanza, the trope of "time to breathe" has become instead a metaphor for the swift passing of time: "in the time / it takes to breathe he too is gone forever."

The next section takes us back to the poet's own past, and to his work on the crab boat in Alaska. The stanzas are slightly longer here (nine lines instead of seven), although the steady pulse of the iambic pentameter remains constant. We are told, "There was another ship, another time, / but going nowhere." This image, together with details of the way the ship "tugged like a leashed dog with boundless hope / but never left the shore," provides a powerful metaphor for the experiences of the workers on board the ship, who "felt time rising from the gray stack." In the final stanza of this section, the poet brings together in suggestive fashion images already evoked in the poem:

> A current stirs the trees like tidal grass.
> Stand in the kitchen looking out to sea
> through stands of waving limbs and feel the wind,
> the leaking vessels of the blood go down.

The final section consists of three quatrains, each presenting a series of brief statements about the passing of time. The last two stanzas are in the future tense, however, and while they seem to indicate, in Ozymandias fashion, the inexorable cancelation wrought by time ("The ruined millionaire will watch his house / tip like a sandbox toy and slide away"—an image that recalls an earlier poem about changes in life, "The Lost House"), the third stanza (the only one to rhyme in the poem) concludes the poem with images that suggest an inrush of high-spirited Yeatsian energy:

> A colony of ants will have its say
> remembered by the beetle rolling dung.
> An old man dances, knowing he is young.
> A woman dances in the breaking day.

It is an extraordinary poem, ranging as it does over Mason's life and echoing some of his earlier works, both in prose and verse. It suggests an awareness of a turning point in his life.

The next poem in the book, set in New Mexico, is a pantoum, **"Gallina Canyon,"** in which the repeated lines in each stanza effectively convey the sensation of unremitting repetitive noise, which is the subject of the poem:

> All night the cattle bellowed,
> cows and calves of the separated herd
> seeking each other under helpless stars,
> never sleeping, even when the dog slept.

The effect is overwhelming, and when we reach the final stanza, the second and fourth lines turn out to be the first and third lines of the opening stanza, suggesting that distress is an inescapable condition.

The poem that follows, **"Saying Grace,"** is a fourteen-line lyric, arranged in two rhyming stanzas of iambic trimeter. In its evocation of "The silence of a night / of supplicating stars," it almost appears to be an answering prayer to the clamorous despair of the previous poem. It has something of the reverence for the ways of nature to be found in the poetry of Wendell Berry—for example, "The Peace of Wild Things," which also evokes "the grace of the world." The final two lines of Mason's poem are extremely moving in their simple supplication:

> Give us this day more world
> than we can ever know.

It serves also as an introductory lyric to a series of poems celebrating the wild nature of North America, from the "scarred and twisted beauty" of **Bristlecone Pine** to "the grass / banks where the buffalo graze" of **To the Sea of Cortez** and the "muscled force of air" of a heron that beats above the poet's head in **The Secret Hearing.** In the last of these poems, the memory of the primitive force of the great bird in its sudden flight ("Big as a pterodactyl and as old / it seemed") offers a quasi-religious remedy for an otherwise unsatisfactory life (the poem appears to recall an episode from Mason's early days as a gardener, during his unhappy first marriage); however, as yet he was only capable of "half-worshipping the world that made such flight," and so it had to remain a "hidden music in [his] lungs," drowned out by "the sound / of the diesel engine" of his tractor.

The poem that follows, "**Mending Time**," in unrhyming tercets, seems to riff on Frost's "Mending Wall," beginning as it does with the short sentence "The fence was down." But whereas Frost's poem presents a meditation on the value of or need for fences, Mason's recalls an episode from the past in which the speaker had gone out with others to bring back sheep that had strayed on account of a toppled fence. The nighttime search in the moonlight is evoked with dreamlike details:

> Then we saw
> the weather of white wool, a cloud in the blue
>
> moving without sound as if charmed
> by the moon beholding them out of bounds.

The final lines switch to the present tense, informing us that "Time has not tightened the wire or righted the barn," making the poem's title seem somewhat ironic. In the final tercet, the mysterious effects of the remembered moonlight are substituted by "sunlight creeping back / like a song with nobody left to hear it." We are again reminded of some of Robert Frost's poems, in particular those that describe and commemorate farms that have gone to ruin, as in "The Need of Being Versed in Country Things" or "Directive."

The next cluster of poems takes us across the ocean to Europe, being set in Great Britain, Greece, and Spain. "**Across the Pyrenees**" reports a memory of a journey on a night train to Spain, in the 1970s when "Franco was still alive." The ballad-like stanzas of rhyming tetrameter are suited to the subject matter, which is a simple but charming evocation of a moment of received generosity, with the young traveler being taught how to drink from a *bota:*

> He showed me how to tip my head
> and squeeze the skin until a line
>
> of fruit and sunlight filled my mouth
> with a sweat and leather aftertaste.

The poem strikes by its narrative essentiality—as economic and plain in its details as is the meal the passengers share: "bread / and wine, cheese and fruit." And the final stanza makes it clear that the poem has no pretensions beyond testifying to a memorable moment in the narrator's life:

> Yes—it happened many years ago
> in the passing dark of northern Spain.
> Some strangers shared their food with me
> in the dim light of the night train.

This poem is followed by six highly accomplished translations of Greek poetry, which lead into another memory from Mason's early European travels, "**First Christmas in the Village.**" This poem, in unrhyming six-line stanzas, once again has at its heart a memory of simple but exotic food, the speaker's first taste of octopus: "It tasted like a briny steak / with tentacles like tiny lips / oozing the savor of the sea." But the prevailing image is that of fire amidst the darkness, which also serves to convey the sense of treasured companionship—a feeling of warmth that the speaker is able to take back to his lonely "rented dwelling":

> That night I carried a bucket of coals
> back to my rented dwelling, wind
> trailing the fading sparks behind—
> a small fire, for the warmth it made
> as the stars held steady in the dome,
> and sleep became an open grave.

The next two poems take us to colder northern climes. Yet these poems are more dreamlike in their movement— the second one is titled "The Nightmare Version"—and they do not describe specific moments from the past but instead conjure emotional atmospheres. **"Given Rain"** is written in short-lined quatrains, with no regular rhyming scheme but with a good deal of assonance (we recall Mason's declaration in the author's note that he catches "vowels more than consonants, so the sound [he] follow[s] is watery") and internal rhyming:

> The world is wet
>
> and close and the light
> is low, the books
> glow with a darkness of their own,
> the words like rain in the mind.

The poem as a whole has an incantatory effect, suggesting the almost magical power that books can have on the imagination of children. Given the rainy setting of the poem, and the evocation of childish imaginativeness, one wonders whether the poem might have been a lyric originally intended for *Davey McGravy*. Read in this light, the rather mysterious title becomes meaningful: rain can be considered a gift if it spurs a child to travel the roads of literature, and hence to nourish his or her imaginative powers.

"The Nightmare Version," as one might expect from the title, is a rather more unsettling poem. It is written in *terza rima* stanzas of pithy trimeter (with a certain amount of slant-rhyming). The reference to a "pint of bitter" and the use of the word "kirkyard" suggest that the poem has its origins in Mason's early travels to Scotland in search of family connections. As the title hints, however, rather than offering an account of a specific event in the speaker's past, the poem evokes through metaphorical means a general sense of foreboding and disgust. While fire was the recurring image in his poem about the Greek village, this poem is steeped in dampness—but there is nothing baptismal or inspiring about this watery immersion. The poem begins and ends with a drowned pig; rain is not a gift from heaven but something that soaks the visitor's clothes, and beer, although providing momentary solace, also stains the floor. A mirror provides no sense of illumination or reflection but rather seems to have trapped the visitor's face in its "glint," giving us the sense that the earlier visit mentioned in the penultimate stanza ("because you've been here before") is part of a recurring pattern, like endlessly repeating reflections in mirrors.

It is followed by another short poem in rhyming tercets (this time with insistent triple rhymes), "**Daytime,**"
which captures the sense of disorientated alienation that
large hotels, with their ubiquitous screens, can arouse in
the visitor. The whole poem consists of a single sentence,
whose subject ("I") does not appear until the third tercet.
The sense of alienation is conveyed in two metaphors; one
is drawn from computer technology, while the other is a
far more traditional poetic trope: "and feeling pixelated, /
dust in a sunbeam [...]." The poem ends with the speaker
wondering whether "a particle, afloat / can teach itself to
pray, or to devote / its substance to the god of the remote."
The last few words again merge contemporary technology
with a sense of something more primitive.

"**To Hygeia,**" which is in unrhyming hexameter, could
be considered an attempt to create a contemporary Homeric hymn. It is addressed to the goddess of health and
combines memories of childhood and meditations on ap-
proaching old age. At its heart is a simple memory of a
child's encounters with an "old man with a tinkling high-
ball," who would orate, *When I was a boy* [...]" As the
poet now ruefully realizes, "the lesson I failed to get was
the one / he always meant: *One of these days, you smug twit,
/ you'll be me.*" In the poem, he wittily—but also touchingly—passes from beautifully detailed memories of the old
people he had assisted in his youth—"I chauffeured the
old, cajoled them to keep up the work of living, / helped
them to their doors, found keys, conveyed them / to

dough-smelling kitchens, pans of foiled leftovers […]" — to lists of his own ailments and medications, concluding:

> Now I've only to hallow their too-neglected names
> with yours, goddess, each time I offer a lit candle
> or swallow the pills and pride or raise my ringing glass.

The zeugma in the last line subtly plays on the poem's constant shifts from past to present, and from detached observation to personal (and painful) experience.

The next two poems, "**The New Dope**" and "**Disturbed Paradelle**," both appear to be attempts to capture disturbed states of mind. The first one, in irregular couplets, with intermittent internal rhymes and echoes, describes an experience with a new drug. The return to normality is symbolized by "this // abyss-less ordinary mug / of coffee in my hands," rather as in "The Gifts of Time." The second poem is an experiment in the form invented by Billy Collins; with its repetitions and broken phrases, it seems to have been placed deliberately on the facing page to "The New Dope."

There follows a trio of poems that draw on Native American myths and history, in particular, the painful history of relations between the Indigenous peoples of North America and the white settlers. The first of the trio, "**The Great Changer**," is a sonnet mainly in rhyming couplets with a steady iambic beat, which confers a somewhat ritualistic tone on the short narrative. It proceeds mainly by repeated negatives: "She was not Salmon Woman swimming under fog. // She was not Echo, nor was she Talking River […]" It is not until the final rhyming couplet that we finally reach an affirmative: "But she was Fox and found her gnawed-off limb / and the Great Changer came. And she welcomed him." Mason has indicated that the poem is about his mother and her addiction, using the Lummi Indian tropes of people she worked with when he was young.

This sonnet, which possibly draws on Hermann Haeberlin's collection of Indian tales from Puget Sound, is followed by another short poem, titled "**Horse People**," which in two highly compressed stanzas recount the story of the mother of Quanah Parker, known as "the last Chief of the Comanche." Each stanza, respectively of eight and seven lines, consists of a single sentence; what is extraordinary is the amount of poignant history that Mason succeeds in packing into these two sentences. The first sentence begins with the backstory of the mother's life, with the hectic story of her kidnapping as a child, which is rendered in concentrated but vivid images—"thrown on the hurtling rump / of a warrior's pony whipped to the far off / and utterly unwritten Comancheria." It is not until line six that the principal clause arrives—"the little blonde began her life"—which is immediately followed by the apparently paradoxical statement "outcast / only when the whites recaptured her." The tragic truth of this is immediately explained by the details that follow: "and killed / the man she loved, the father of her children."

The second stanza takes us beyond the plain facts of

her life to her place in history and public opinion ("The language she forgot would call her ruined / and beyond redemption [...]"), while also continuing the history into the next generation. The poem tells us of her son "who died in comforts his mother spurned" but concludes with the memory that he shared with her of "how the manes / of the remuda caught the breezes as they ran, / and how the grass caught fire in the scalp-red sun." These final images are striking in their suggestive power, testifying to the dramatic beauty of the landscape but also gesturing back to the scenes of violence with which the poem opened.

The poem that follows, "**Sand Creek**," apparently describes a landscape—that of southeastern Colorado—but actually evokes all the horror of a massacre that took place there: a slaughter of Cheyenne and Arapaho people by the US Army in 1864. The poem is organized in thirteen free-verse couplets, with no punctuation except for occasional commas. After two couplets describing the land and the sky, with startling similes ("The land flayed open like a skin / on which the stories would be drawn"), the narrator (who mentions himself only once, in line nine) focuses on small, disconnected details, adding to the impression of a wounded and fragmented landscape:

> I bend a knee
> and lean on shatterings of rock
>
> or watch a beetle right itself
> and struggle into stems and weeds

> a cricket like an autumn leaf
> crackling in crooked light

It seems impossible to make sense of this damaged land, where "there is blood, blood everywhere." The final couplet returns us to the opening image of the land as skin, but the grim suggestion seems to be that the stories written thereon have in fact left no permanent mark: "the skin / with its evaporating stain."

The next two poems offer a certain respite from the tragedies of American history. "**Frangipani,**" in five un-rhyming tercets, appears to be the first Australian poem in the volume, as indicated in the reference to the Southern Cross. It introduces a welcome note of color and perfume into the collection, even while acknowledging the fragility of this beauty, since the poem is actually describing "Cut blossoms floating in a bowl of water," which "are what they are." Nonetheless, we are told that to know these "fragile blooms / with breathing color is to be reborn / astir, astray, and happier than before." The poem ends on an ambiguous note:

> So let the sphinx moths hunting nectar there
> where none exists be go-betweens for life,
> purposefully duped. Let the perfume rise.

This refers to the fact that sphinx moths are deceived into keeping frangipani alive, pollenating the flowers by searching for nectar that they do not contain. In this case, the duping is perhaps double, since these "cut blossoms" are no longer alive anyway. But they can still emanate perfume—and the poet can still celebrate this, as he does in the final words, like a simple prayer.

"**Galahs in the Wind**," in four unrhyming quatrains, celebrates the clamor and clatter of the commonest of Australian cockatoos—and also its destructive habit of tearing leaves: "Oh joy, the limbs and leaves / are tearing like the waves." The poem, apparently written in the voice of a galah, uses synesthesia and raucous onomatopoeia to capture the vigor and hubbub of the birds: "The sunlight shouts and we // *tsup-tsup* in riotous flight." An online urban dictionary reports that one possible meaning of *tsup* is that of an alternative to *mwah*, to render the idea of a kiss. The final stanza, with its characteristically assonantal exhortation ("at once we must, we must / *tsup-tsup* to the sun"), recalls the pagan hymn of "boisterous devotion to the sun" in the penultimate stanza of "Sunday Morning" by Stevens, another poet famously fond of self-coined onomatopoeic words.

The next three poems return to family memories. The first one, "**My Scottish Grandmother's Lobotomy**," announces its tragic subject in the title. It tells the story in three nine-line stanzas, each line consisting of precisely seven syllables. The mathematical precision of the syllabic verse seems to underscore the shocking nature of the story recounted. It begins with the line "The tool used hardly mattered," a disconcerting statement after the title. The "procedure" is described in apparently matter-of-fact fashion, as if in a manual of instructions, and we learn that the intent was to deal with states of emotional disturbance—or what were seen as such: "flights of high / or crashing spirits." The tragic outcome is depicted in the last stanza, with "[t]he mad girl / wrecked and pinioned in a bed." It is not until the last two lines that the narrator's personal involvement, as indicated in the title, is made manifest: "I never heard her accent, / her laughter, even a cough."

The next poem, "**Bildungsroman**," which is dedicated to the memory of Seamus Heaney, is an unrhyming sonnet that recounts a simple episode from Mason's childhood that, as he puts it, gave him "a shock of the real." This came about through his desire "to see beyond," climbing up the metal ladder to the top bunk in order to see the night train that "threw the forest shadows / spinning across our bedroom wall"—which is to say, "to see the light / that cast the passing images." The child's curiosity leads to his sticking his "foot / right through the bedroom window glass"—and the subsequent mockery by his brother "for trying / to see beyond." The dedication to Heaney would seem to invite us to see in the poem a metaphor for poetic exploration of the world and poetic vision, as in such poems by Heaney as "The Skylight" (*Seeing Things*). In Heaney's poetry, as so often in Mason's, such transcendental yearnings are balanced by a literally earthy realism, represented in Mason's sonnet by the brother's derisory response (a reaction that may remind us of what happens in *Davey McGravy*).

"**Hangman**," in four rhyming tetrameter sextains, again includes the poet's elder brother, who here taunts his sibling with his superior verbal skills. The elder brother knows a new word that "starts with *d* and rhymes with *force*." This word is deliberately never spelled out in the poem. The careful rhyming structure of the poem mirrors the elaborate spelling game the two boys are playing, which works as the central metaphor for the destructive force that is going to upset the children's lives:

> I let myself be hanged, and learn
> a new word whispered out of fear,
> though it will be another year
> before I feel the house cut loose,
> my dangling body and the burn
> of shame enclosing like a noose.

The next poem, "**Security Light**," in four unrhymed hexameter tercets, starts with the image of "the glow outside our window," which is "no fallen star" but rather "the fear of night / a neighbor burns with, nightmare of a stubborn child." The tercets that follow instead recount the narrator's own dream of the dark, which at first sight might also appear to be a nightmare: "I dreamed of chasing crows in a dark of sea fog [...]." But it proves itself rather to be a vision of the dark sea as a symbol of "changing things," and hence of time: "the moving sand clock of the sea." The power of the poem lies in the striking images it presents of the ceaseless processes of movement and change:

I saw the waters running out to meet the water
coming in, the small crabs lifted off their claws.
I saw the trysting place of cormorants, the cliffs

of guarded nests where eagles watched like sated kings
alive [...]

This poem is followed by a moving poem in tercets in memory of a student who committed suicide, "**The Student**," and a poem in rhyming tetrameter quatrains, "**Old Man Walking**," the Frostian quality of which John Greening commented on in the *Times Literary Supplement*, stating that it "might as easily be called 'Acquainted with the Day.'" The poem was indeed first published in the *Robert Frost Review*. Here is the final stanza:

An old man never walks alone.
Let others judge what others see.
The old man walking on the road
had words to keep him company.

The next poem, "**Passion**," is an unusual one for Mason, Whitman-like in its long anaphoric lines of free verse and its list of fondly observed details: "and it isn't the lovely rapture of the cellist who, between her legs and in the fluent embrace of her arms, / gives birth to a god who makes the audience tremble [...]." The poem describes a performance of Bach's *St Matthew Passion*, essentially celebrating the uniqueness of the moment. After nine long lines making up a single sentence, each separate clause beginning with "It isn't ...", the last line contains three sentences: "It is all of them. And it passes. And will never be heard again on earth."

The brief poem (twelve lines) on the facing page is rather like a comic reversal of "Passion," offering a satirical portrayal of a poetry reading in which political passion is presumed to be all that is needed to "turn opinions into art." It ends with a final couplet, the rhyme of which was criticized (in an otherwise favorable review) by John Greening:

"One longs for a quiet thought / no one applauds / and words that are not clods." Even ignoring the elliptical grammar and the half-rhyme on "words," "not clods" is hard to accept.

The criticism seems unwarranted; it seems perfectly in keeping with the satirical intent of the poem that the final word of this poem should be an unforgettably clunky monosyllable, reproducing the very effect that the speaker is lampooning.

The poem that follows, "**Michael Donaghy 1954–2004**," pays homage to a poet of a different sort. Elsewhere, Mason has described Donaghy as being "among the very best of my generation" (*Two Minds*, 138). The poem consists of just four lines:

Like a wash of paint on board, transparent figures,
unsolid as shadows and the passing river ...
I look at them, and look again, again—
a lifetime passing in a shower of rain.

In his essay on the New Formalist movement, Mason described how Donaghy's shorter poems "demonstrate how lightly he wore the mantle of mastery."

The penultimate poem in the section devoted to new work, **"We Stand Together Talking,"** is a ghazal, a form that Mason had adopted in a poem titled "Mumbai" (in *Arrivals*, included in *The Sound*). Whereas in the earlier poem he used the repetends to convey the impression of an excess of sensory stimulation, here the recurring trisyllabic rhymes (beginning with "making love") play on the precarious persistence of love in a world of violence and hate. At the end of the ghazal, the last words of the couplet are respectively "hate" and "love."

> My love, the harm was hidden, but the hate
> would damn us living for the sake of love.

But this disconcerting equilibrium is perhaps countered by the fact that "love" opens and closes the couplet—and also by the fact that the final rhyme of the whole poem, "for the sake of love," is almost identical to the opening rhyme: "forsaken love." And in this rhyme, at least, negative has been turned to positive.

The final poem is another single quatrain that bears the simple title **"Epigram."** It both brings this section to a strong conclusion (once again with a powerful aquatic image) and serves as an opening to the rest of the book. It is as if we, as readers, are being invited to surrender to the current of feeling. As is appropriate in such a book, this short poem looks both backward and forward: this volume is not just the cap on an already successful career but also heralds a new beginning for Mason. Now retired from academia, he has embarked on a new literary life on a new continent. Everything suggests that it is going to be a vigorous and exciting one.

> The baby's bawling and the old man's laughter
> rise from the center of the same *I am*.
> Say it to windows, doors. Say it to rafters
> on rivers of light. Say it to the breaking dam.

CHAPTER 11

Interview

The following interview was conducted via email in two phases, the first part in March 2013 and the second in October 2021.

March 2013

GD: *Do you make a conscious distinction between poetry that is personal—closely connected with your own life—and poetry that is fictional in content?*

DM: I honestly don't know the difference most of the time, Gregory. I mean, I know I have written poems that are "true" to a memory, true to the basic facts, but everything in the poem is done for the sake of the poem, and besides, I never know whether anyone's memory is accurate or not. Ultimately, I just treat poems as poems, no matter where they come from. Both Hobbes and Joyce said that memory and imagination were the same thing. I agree.

GD: *If you are asked about the personal circumstances behind some of your poems—the breakup of your family, for example, or marital crises—do you consider such questions as reasonable or as an intrusion—or perhaps just irrelevant?*

DM: Funny, isn't it, this biographical interest? Knowing Elizabeth Bishop's life changes the way we read the poems. Is that a good thing? Well, yes and no. A poem that is really working well will tell as much about the reader as the author. It will have a body of its own, and that body has to be seen and felt. But no knowledge, biographical or otherwise, is out of bounds. Perhaps we're trained to think biographical readings inappropriate in part because we know so little about some writers and think we can focus purely on their poems. We think ourselves virtuous for doing so. Notions of virtue are always suspect in my opinion. Reading and writing are partly a conversation, and gossip is not all bad in such a context. As for me, I don't give a fig what other people know, as long as what they judge my poems by has some basis in reality.

GD: *Do you think of yourself primarily as a narrative poet?*

DM: Nearly every poem tells a story in some way, or contains voices in conflict. Due to my history as a prose fiction writer, it came naturally to me to tell stories in verse, but my failure as a fiction writer might be tied somehow to a deeper lyric impulse. Maybe I am really a dramatic poet. No matter what kind of poem I am writing, the human presence, or what I have called "dramatic voice," is deeply important. Voices in conflict, voices in extremis—maybe that's what I am about. Maybe opera is reminding me to be a playwright!

GD: *And yet* Ludlow *has far less dramatic voice than your other narratives. Was it a conscious decision on your part to move away from the dramatic monologue for this work? Or was it just inevitable, given the length of the book?*

DM: Quite conscious, and quite liberating. I wanted the freedom of a kind of omniscient narration—thinking of writers I love like Lawrence and Woolf. But I don't agree that the poem lacks dramatic voice as I conceive of it. The narrator is a character, after all, and you are never not in the presence of a human being. Still, I remember feeling exhilarated by the freedom I felt to tell the story from multiple points of view and to move about in time and location as freely as I did.

GD: *I understand* Ludlow *is to become an opera, too. How will this work? Will you eliminate the role of the narrator?*

DM: I've now spent years thinking about this, and before I wrote the libretto for the opera of *Ludlow*, I often asked readers what they thought of that narrator. Ultimately, I decided to keep him. The composer, Lori Laitman, likes what he gives her for musical possibilities, and our stage director, Beth Greenberg, has a lot of ideas for changing the narrator's relationship to the story as it moves along. We call him the "Poet" in the opera.

I have streamlined the story in other ways—its chronology is tighter—and have developed a love story for Louis and Luisa that does not exist in the book. This is opera, after all. They have a great duet in jail. I've used fewer major characters, though still a large cast with three small choruses that become one chorus at the climactic battle.

Act One of the opera has been set to music and staged in a workshop production by the fine musicians at the University of Colorado in Boulder. Lori is at work scoring Act Two (there are three in all). The libretto is "finished," though I always make small changes as Lori needs them for musical purposes. I think it has the potential of being a great American opera.

GD: *You haven't written any other long narratives since* Ludlow. *Is this because your energies have gone into libretto writing? Do you see yourself writing another verse novel?*

DM: The late Hayden Carruth urged me to write another epic. He was very enthusiastic about what I had done.

I have had a story in the back of my mind, as it were, but these things lie inert for years before a galvanizing energy sets them in motion. I have to trust this part of the process. I have to wait and see, and in the meantime, there are so many projects in the works.

I think I actually *have* written another verse novel, or a series of linked stories, which was first conceived as a children's book but might prove to be a book for readers of all ages. This is called *Davey McGravy*—a nickname my father gave me, and which my wife, Chrissy, saw was rich with poetic possibilities. A boy who has lost his mother in a mysterious and unexplained fog is given a rhyming nickname as a gesture of love by his father, and it sets him off on a series of encounters with the natural world, seeing correspondences—rhymes—everywhere. Some people think it's the best book I have ever done, and I am inclined to agree. So it will be interesting finding the right illustrator and publisher for it. One has to be patient with these things.

Meanwhile, I've got my best collection of shorter poems coming out in 2014, *Sea Salt: Poems of a Decade*, and the opera work isn't drying up. I've just written a one-act libretto for Music of Remembrance in Seattle called *After Life*, which is about Picasso and Stein and the manner in which they managed to survive World War II. I shouldn't say more about that yet, but I am very proud of the libretto's tragi-comic tone.

GD: *In your narrative poetry, are you influenced in any way by contemporary prose novelists or are the influences primarily poetical ones?*

DM: Other than Frost and Jeffers, neither of whom could do naturalistic dialogue, and perhaps as well Hecht and Walcott, I can't say my narrative influences are poets. Fiction writers—Tolstoy, Chekhov, Maupassant, Hemingway, Faulkner, [Cormac] McCarthy, DeLillo, [Philip] Roth, Twain, Bierce, Cather, Woolf, Joyce, Lawrence,

Borges—I have learned from all of these. All of them. And Homer, too, of course.

GD: *I have never thought of you as particularly drawn to the Romantics, perhaps with the exception of Byron, given the connection with Auden. For that reason, I was curious to come across your poem "Mrs Mason and the Poets." Was it just the surname that drew you to this topic?*

DM: I think I went through a rather anti-Romantic phase in my earlier years, partly under the influence of Auden, but now I am in fact devoted to them, and I have taught Romantic poetry classes several times. I adore Keats to distraction—the letters as well as the poems. I am a huge admirer of Blake, whom my wife knows far better than I do. I confess I go hot and cold over Wordsworth but am constantly forced to acknowledge his greatness. Indeed, the best of Wordsworth just shatters me every time I read it. The "Immortality Ode," "Michael," "Resolution and Independence," and quite a few other works. And I feel deep attachment to a handful of Coleridge poems. I think *The Rime of the Ancient Mariner* is just one of the gems of the language and one of the very best examples of narrative we have. I adore "Frost at Midnight" and a handful of other poems. And I am learning to love more Shelley than I used to love. In fact, it was while reading a superb biography of Shelley by Edmund Blunden that I came up with the idea for that dramatic monologue about "Mrs. Mason"—the assumed name of an Irish aristocrat who knew Byron and Shelley well.

It's a great blessing that one changes one's allegiances over the course of a reading life. I'd hate to be so stuck in my opinions that I couldn't be persuaded to see a poet in a different way. That's probably the best thing about teaching—it forces me to reread and revise my judgments.

GD: *Greece and Greek culture are clearly very important to you. Do you feel the direct influence of Greek literature, whether classical or contemporary?*

DM: Utterly. The dramatists, especially Aeschylus, Sophocles, and Euripides, have meant the world to me. Homer is essential to me. Classicist friends know what I borrowed from Homer for *Ludlow*. The classical lyric poets and medieval song writers as well. The modern Greek poets have also meant much to me. I have much Seferis memorized and can sing his verses. I know Cavafy very well, Elytis slightly less so, and Sikelianos, and quite a few others, including my dear friend Yiorgos Chouliaras, whose work I have co-translated. Let's see, I have translated Palamas, Seferis, Cavafy, Ritsos, Chouliaras, and some others as yet unpublished. Those are big, big influences. I have also been influenced by Katerina Anghelaki-Rooke, though I have never managed to translate her successfully. I think it's her giant personality that has touched me most.

GD: *Do you think of yourself as a New Formalist? Does the term mean anything?*

DM: I always thought the name was idiotic and have said so in print. First of all, formalism by itself is insufficient for art. Second of all, nothing really good is all that new. Novelty is crap. Accuracy and authenticity come first. I do not give a damn about being new. I give a damn about being precise and beautiful and memorable. Most American poets trying to be new just end up writing dull prose—I don't see why they bother. And most so-called formalist poems never get beyond fulfilling the rules of a given form—there's no life in them. The best poets in any form are fresh and vital and unkillable, unforgettable. That's what matters, not conforming to anyone's party affiliation. I coedited the first big "New Formalist" anthology and wrote most of the introduction for it, but that was a job. I was fine with leaving my own work out of it. My essay called "The Limits of the Literary Movement" says much about this.

GD: *How do you choose the forms of your poetry?*

DM: I don't. I have never written a good poem by choosing the form first. Ever. Forms find me. They help me along. I don't go looking for them. I work by instinct and call up everything I know when I write a poem, and I never know what will come to my aid.

GD: *In your libretti, one obvious model (whom you acknowledge) is Auden. Are there others? Do you see yourself as continuing along this path?*

DM: I have learned from Gioia and McClatchy as well. But I am not an authority on opera, as they are. I do have a good dramatic sense and a good sense of what might be singable. I've done a lot of acting and singing. And I know how to make a scene. In more ways than one. The work is enormous fun and I get paid for it, and both of those things are important considerations. There's also the joy of collaboration, watching a composer go to town with my words, watching singers and musicians and stage directors at work. I love the theatre almost as much as I love solitude.

GD: *You have won acclaim as a teacher. How important is teaching for you?*

DM: The teaching life is a blessing, albeit sometimes a mixed one. I love nearly all of my students, and I think it is an honor and a privilege to teach. It is wonderful to be involved with great writing in the classroom, to be allowed to enthuse as one wishes over beautiful lines and sentences. I like to think I have turned on a few lightbulbs in the last twenty-odd years. But I would retire tomorrow if I had the money. I always wanted first and foremost to be a writer. All my life. I would write full time if I had the chance and have always been happiest when not going to a job. I have been very, very fortunate in my teaching positions, my colleagues, etc. But I have a lot of work still to do and precious little time to do it in. Think of Keats: "When I have fears that I may cease to be," and all that. Hell, I'm more than twice his age and still I worry my pen will never glean my teeming brain. There's just so much to be done!

GD: *You are one of the best critics of contemporary poetry around. Do you do your critical writing for love or money?*

DM: Thanks for saying so. I've really lost a lot of confidence in myself as a critic—probably a good thing, since I used to make dismissive judgments far too easily. To be perfectly honest, most contemporary poetry is so profoundly boring that I can't bear to review it. I would rather die. But yes, I do reviews for the money. I mean, I have editor friends I don't want to disappoint, but I really do write reviews for the money. If I did not need money, I would not write reviews. I wish I could write more of another kind of literary essay, a kind of essay I have dabbled in, and I hope to get to that sort of thing more concertedly one day. All in good time. I'm looking back at that adage I just typed: All in good time. What a wonderful thing to say. Wouldn't it be nice if everything was all in good time?

GD: *You are now married to a poet. Do you work together? Do you think your wife's poetry has influenced yours?*

DM: Let me be frank. I do not think there is a poet writing in English today who has more talent than Cally Conan-Davies, whom I know as Chrissy Mason. I do not say that idly. When her work is finally seen, it will astonish anyone who can read. I have been a professional judge of poetry for thirty years. I mean it. I cannot think of anyone who brings more experience urgently to bear in beautiful language than she does, and I can quote from memory examples to prove my point. Editors are now catching up with this poet's talent and publishing her in the best magazines the language has to offer. So that's my first statement. I believe in her poems as much as I believe in anyone's, including my own.

When I read most contemporary poetry, I find it wooden, almost wholly without music, the very quality she has in abundance, as well as the courage to write the unsayable. I aspire to learn from her.

Yes, we work together. I make suggestions about her poems, and she challenges me right to my very foundations to make things better in both poetry and prose. She is one tough editor and reader, and suffers not the slightest folly. Everything I have done since meeting her has been improved by her scrutiny. It's thrilling to me. I like to think I have been influenced by her, but I am not sure yet how to say what the influence might be, except that I have written a lot of love poems.

GD: *Can you see yourself and Chrissy working on a joint project?*

DM: Our whole life is a joint project. We collaborate on *everything*. So far, we have written one poem together, and I am sure there will be many more, but I can absolutely see us writing books together.

GD: *Have you also discovered the world of Australian poetry as a result of this change in your life? Or were you already familiar with it?*

DM: I have long been an admirer of A. D. Hope and

lately am pretty rapturous over certain poems by Les Murray. I knew some of James McAuley, Judith Wright, Gwen Harwood but have learned more of their work since falling in love with Chrissy. One huge revelation she produced for me regards the poetry of Kenneth Slessor, whom I did not know at all. Hearing Chrissy read to me his great poem "Five Bells" was one of the most sublime experiences of my life. So, yes, Australian poetry is becoming more and more important to me. We've lately been introduced to the song writer and poet Joe Dolce, an American living in Oz, and I hope he will connect us to much more in the arts world over there.

I should add that long before I knew Chrissy, I was a fan of Australian fiction and films. We're hoping I can teach a course over there in the next few years. Much planning to be done.

GD: *How do you think your poetry has changed over the years?*

DM: Well, my first book was very much a journeyman effort. Enough said. My second is a real book, my third a better one. From *Arrivals* forward, I think you are generally in the hands of someone who knows what he is doing. Maybe *The Country I Remember* too. But since that time my work has been more charged, more passionate, more memorable. I think my next book, *Sea Salt*, is obviously the best thing I have done, along with *Ludlow, Davey Mc-Gravy*, and the *libretti*. If I ever do a "New and Selected," I will include little if any of the early work. I am the proverbial late bloomer, and now I think I am really hitting my stride.

October 2021:
Picking Up Where We Left Off

GD: *I see that in your as yet unpublished new collection,* Pacific Light, *you have revised an earlier poem of yours, "New Zealand Letter," in memory of Anne Stevenson. Is this something you are tempted to do with other poems? Or is this just a one-off occasion, prompted by the death of your friend? (It is a poem I'm particularly fond of, so I was glad to see it resuscitated, after you had omitted it from* The Sound.*)*

DM: As the years go by, I'm increasingly impressed by poets like Derek Mahon, who continually revised his earlier work. Yeats did as well. Mahon's revisions were not always improvements, and one of Yeats's, "Brown Penny," was also not an improvement. But the process of revisiting an earlier poem is still inviting, and in the context of the new collection, I felt this one would work well. I hope I've done it justice.

GD: *You were very selective in your choices from your early volumes in* The Sound, *though I was glad to see you spared the longer narratives for the most part. But your most recent collections have had fewer narratives. Are you no longer tempted by the genre? Is prose narrative attracting you more (I mean as a writer, not a reader)?*

DM: As you know, I have been trying to write prose fiction again after many years away from it. My first motive was to see if I could make some money, but the jury's out on that score. There are still some narrative bits in the new book of poems—"The Suicide's House," etc.—but none is really extended into the arc of a story. A poem called "The End of Stories" suggests despite its ambiguous title that stories are still out there, alive and catchable. I'd like to catch a few more of them in verse, if time allows. I'm also publishing a new book of essays, several of which involve narrative, and my introduction to the book avows that I'm really more a storyteller than anything else. That seems right to me.

GD: *The huge change in your life has been your move to Australia. In terms of your writing, does this just mean a change of background? Different natural sights to describe, for example ... Or is it something more profound?*

DM: I'm just reviewing a new book, *Into the Rip*, by the *New York Times* correspondent Damien Cave, who set up a bureau in Sydney and has lived there about four years now. Cave uses the Australian culture of surfing and life-saving to meditate on cultural differences between Australia and the US. The differences are profound. Whatever diffidence Australians may feel about their country, whatever problems exist (and they do exist, especially with the conservatives in power), they have still made a more cohesive and agreeable society than that of my native country. So the simple answer to your question is that this is an ideal place to live out my last years, a country with fewer guns and better health care and some really wonderful people, many of them immigrants.

But there's another element to living here. This is an old, old continent. Remnants of Gondwanaland still exist in the Tasmanian wilderness. Australian Aboriginal society is the oldest continuous human civilization on earth, at least 65,000 years old. Every dawn in Australia, at least outside the cities, feels like the beginning of the world. The dawn chorus of Australian birds is one of the most beautiful things I have ever witnessed. So I feel as if I have come to a place with just a hint of familiarity—Tasmania resembles the northwestern American landscapes I grew up in—and plenty that is new (and old) to learn. Each day on waking, I open the curtains and say a thanks to whatever gods are listening for letting me be here.

I have much new history to learn. Tasmania has its dark side too, its wounds, but these are not unlike the historical troubles I grew up with in America. So one is continually grappling with what it means to be a human being, why there is evil in the world, what is the good life—all the big questions seem as present and pressing as ever. My writing life feels richer and more involved, somehow, and surely part of this comes from the fact that I have retired from teaching and don't have to expend my energy on committee work or departmental politics. I can focus on what really matters to me. I'm living the life I always wanted to live, writing as much as I can, but also doing good physical labor on our bit of land. That's the right combination for me, and this is an ideal place to be doing it.

GD: *Is there a lively poetry scene in Tasmania? Do you worry about being cut off?*

DM: Cut off from what? The thing about arts scenes— and Tasmania's is as active as any—is that they take one away from the work and involve one in the social life, which has always been secondary to me. A little social life goes a long way, so we're glad to live an hour's drive from the island's capital, down a winding coastal road of immense beauty. We've met several artists and poets we really admire, and we get up to Hobart or Launceston for concerts, plays, poetry readings, new films—they often show here before they open in the States. Hobart is one of the most beautiful small cities in the world, a mini San Francisco, and I always love my trips up there. The island is packed with bookstores—full of voices, as Caliban might put it. I don't feel we're missing anything culturally—though of course we're not as art-filled as Italy! We are far from some great friends like you, Gregory, but we've been using the various apps to stay in touch.

GD: *I know you have been intrigued by the life of Yeats and have been working on a screenplay about him. One of the poets you have studied very closely, Auden, had a famously cautious attitude toward Yeats, particularly, I think, with regard to the role the Irish poet played as a "sixty-year-old smiling public man." Given that you have been a poet laureate, do you share some of Auden's concerns?*

DM: I always love people who find a way to live life in their own terms. My friend Patrick Leigh Fermor was a great example of this, and Yeats is another. Neither man was channeled through a university education. All the stuff that makes people dislike Yeats—his fascination with aristocracy, his spiritualism, etc.—seems secondary to me. He's just a bloody great lyric poet who can bring the language to a pitch of excitement and interest. Yet, as Auden said, he was a silly man in some ways. My screenplay attempts to show the women who had to endure him and put up with him in his final year, to convey both the greatness of the art and the mere humanity of the man who produced it. A lot of the best poetry by Auden was written before he really made his break with Yeats, and it may be that Auden was too fastidious with his own poems, trimming the great elegy and trying to jettison "September 1, 1939." Larkin, too, moves away from his early Yeats influence. So perhaps Yeats is inimitable, while still offering examples of brilliantly turned poems. I'd like my poems to have the kind of effect the best Yeats poems have, and the best Auden and Larkin and Frost, while remaining themselves. I'd like them to have that kind of staying power.

GD: *Is your interest in poetry and music still an important one?*

DM: Absolutely. If new opera commissions come my way, I will no doubt take them. The last opera I did with Tom Cipullo, "The Parting," premiered in 2018, I think, and is out on CD. Lori Laitman is still working on her opera based on *Ludlow*. Our little house is full of music—we have good speakers that fill the house with sound. And Chrissy (Cally) has taken up the guitar again and is playing beautifully. She wrote her first song for a friend's birthday, and it's a real song. I really wish I played an instrument myself, but every time I think of it, I also think of all the work I haven't done, the books I haven't read, and it doesn't happen. Chrissy got me some wonderful headphones, so at night before sleep I often listen to music from my laptop.

GD: *You have now left the academic world. Is that mainly a relief or do you miss the teaching? (I am sure the students miss you.)*

DM: Students once asked me if I was a teacher who wrote or a writer who taught, and I replied emphatically the latter. I am profoundly glad to be done with it, which does not mean it wasn't an honor to do the work when I did, and of course I loved some of my colleagues and many of my students. Universities have become such unhappy places, with people policing each other's speech and enforcing taste, and administrations cooking up more reasons to elevate fear over trust, that I couldn't recommend anyone aspire to be an academic. My stepdaughter, too, left an academic career in America to eke out a living in Tasmania, and she has never been happier. Setting aside the benefits of salary and long holidays, the effect of academic life in the modern world is to institutionalize everything. Young people think they can't be writers without going to MFA programs, can't be scholars without getting PhDs, so everyone gets ground through the same sausage machine. It turns into a self-fulfilling prophecy, since university graduates publish other university graduates, so people feel left out when they go their own way. Real education, real intellectual life, is a universal good, but in our time the university is not always the location of real intellectual life, and that is worrying.

GD: *How has the pandemic affected you?*

DM: I feel guilty saying this, since I know people who have died in other countries, but we have had it very easy so far in Australia, especially in Tasmania. On this island there have been no COVID cases since about June 2020. We live without masks, with minimal social distancing. We use phone apps to facilitate contact tracing if it becomes needed. We live what used to be called a "normal life." This is an island state, so it's relatively easy for officials to close our border and be done with it. Mostly, this is not a hardship. Tasmanians know they are lucky and know our luck could change at any minute. The vaccine rollout has been slow but is catching up. Now we're becoming aware of the divide that could occur between those who are vaccinated and those who are not. No telling how that will play out. We've read that the death toll in the US has now equaled that of the 1918 pandemic, yet some people still refuse to believe this thing is real and serious.

I said earlier that living here seems to involve me in profound questions about the good life, about life and death. In the end, this pandemic is a great equalizer. We humans are indeed all in the same boat, as it were. Life is dangerous—for some more than for others—and as Auden said, "The sense of danger must not disappear." It's as if Earth is reminding her most arrogant children they are not behaving well and could learn a little humility. Not everyone is capable of learning, and one can only hope those who refuse to learn will not prevail.

Bibliography

Poetry

Small Elegies. Moorhead, MN: Dacotah Territory Press, 1990.
The Buried Houses. Ashland, OR: Story Line Press, 1991.
Land without Grief. Colorado Springs, CO: Jones Alley Press, 1996.
The Country I Remember. Ashland, OR: Story Line Press, 1996.
Arrivals. Ashland, OR: Story Line Press, 2004.
Ludlow: A Verse Novel. Pasadena, CA: Red Hen Press, 2007.
Sea Salt: Poems of a Decade. Pasadena, CA: Red Hen Press, 2014.
Davey McGravy: Tales to Be Read Aloud to Children and Adult Children. Illustrated by Grant Silverstein. Philadelphia, PA: Paul Dry Books, 2015.
The Sound: New and Selected Poems. Pasadena, CA: Red Hen Press, 2018.

Criticism

"The Purposes of Play: A Study of Auden's Longer Poems." PhD diss., University of Rochester, 1989.
The Poetry of Life and the Life of Poetry. Ashland, OR: Story Line Press, 2000.
Two Minds of a Western Poet. Ann Arbor: University of Michigan Press, 2011.
Voices, Places. Philadelphia, PA: Paul Dry Books, 2018.

Memoir

News from the Village. Pasadena, CA: Red Hen Press, 2010.

Opera Libretti

The Scarlet Libretto. Music by Lori Laitman. Pasadena, CA:
Red Hen Press, 2012.
The Scarlet Letter. Music by Lori Laitman. Denver: Opera
Colorado, 2016. [Naxos CD 8669034-35, 2017.]
Vedem. Music by Lori Laitman. Seattle: Northwest Boychoir, 2010.
[Naxos CD 8559685, 2011.]
After Life. Music by Tom Cipullo. Seattle: Music of Remembrance,
2015. [Naxos CD 8669036, 2016.]
The Parting. Music by Tom Cipullo. Seattle: Music of
Remembrance, 2019. [Naxos CD 8669044, 2020.]

Books Edited

Rebel Angels: 25 Poets of the New Formalism. With Mark Jarman.
Ashland, OR: Story Line Press, 1996. [2nd printing, 1999.]
Western Wind: An Introduction to Poetry, 4th ed. With John
Frederick Nims. New York: McGraw-Hill, 2000. [5th ed., 2005.]
Twentieth Century American Poetics. With Dana Gioia and
Meg Schoerke. New York: McGraw-Hill, 2004.
Twentieth Century American Poetry. With Dana Gioia and
Meg Schoerke. New York: McGraw-Hill, 2004.
Poems of the Baca Grande. With Sandra McNew. Colorado Springs,
CO: Hulbert Center Press, 2005.
Contemporary American Poems. General Administration for Press
and Publications of the People's Republic of China (GAPP),
2011.

Bibliography

Further Reading

Allinson, Rayne. "The Poet Immigrant." *FortySouth Tasmania*, May 19, 2021. https://www.fortysouth.com.au/people/the-poet-immigrant.

Anagnostou, Yiorgos. "Poetry Traversing History: Narrating Louis Tikas in David Mason's *Ludlow*." In *Retelling the Past in Contemporary Greek Literature, Film and Popular Culture*, edited by Trine Stauning Willert and Gerasimo Katsan. New York: Lexington Books, 2019.

Brodeur, Brian. "'To Crawl under the Earth': The Persistence of Expansive Poetry." *Hopkins Review* (Winter 2022).

"David Mason Interview with Kaite Hillenbrand." Connotation Press, accessed June 30, 2022. http://connotationpress.com/poetry/563-david-mason-poetry.

"David Mason and His Problems: An Interview with David Rothman." *Able Muse Review* 12 (Winter 2011).

Frisardi, Andrew. "David Mason and the Human Place." *Contemporary Poetry Review*, March 6, 2008. http://www.cprw.com/david-mason-and-the-human-place.

Greening, John. "Bruises Born in Silence: A Distinguished Writer of Restless Narrative." *Times Literary Supplement*, February 22, 2019.

Gwynn, R. S. "Narratives Masonic." *Sewanee Review* 117, no. 1: Winter 2009.

Hix, H. L. "David Mason." In *Dictionary of Literary Biography 282: New Formalist Poets*, edited by Jonathan N. Barron and Bruce Meyer, 207–15. Detroit, MI: Gale, 2003.

Juster, Michael. "Mundane Question." Eratosphere, December 27, 2001. http://www.ablemuse.com/erato/showthread.php?t=5417.

Mason, David. "Dramatic Voice." Eratosphere, August 19, 2004. http://www.ablemuse.com/erato/showthread.php?t=5589.

Waterman, Rory. "David Mason: 'Sea Salt.'" *Times Literary Supplement*, December 12, 2014.

Weste, Linda, ed. *The Verse Novel: Australia and New Zealand*. Melbourne: Australian Scholarly Press, 2021, 231–40.

Works Cited

Hecht, Anthony. *On the Laws of the Poetic Art*. Princeton, NJ: Princeton University Press, 1993.

Hoy, Philip. *Anthony Hecht in Conversation with Philip Hoy*. London: Between the Lines, 1999.

Papanicolas, Zeese. *Buried Unsung: Louis Tikas and the Ludlow Massacre*. Lincoln, NE: University of Nebraska Press, 1982.

Pearce, Roy Harvey. *The Continuity of American Poetry*. Middletown, CT: Wesleyan University Press, 1987.

Shaw, Robert B. "Contrived Corridors." In *The Contemporary Narrative Poem: Critical Crosscurrents*, edited by Steven P. Schneider. Iowa City: University of Iowa Press, 2012.

The Colosseum Critical Introduction to David Mason was designed in
Garamond with Mr Eaves display type and composed by Kachergis Book
Design of Pittsboro, North Carolina. It was printed on 55-pound Maple
Antique Cream and bound by Maple Press of York, Pennsylvania.